Shall I Have Pleasure?

Shall I Have Pleasure?
An Answer for Sarah

Zachary McLeod Hutchins

GREG KOFFORD BOOKS
SALT LAKE CITY, 2025

Greg Kofford Books
P. O. Box 1362
Draper, UT 84020
www.gregkofford.com
facebook.com/gkbooks
twitter.com/gkbooks

———————————————————

Library of Congress Control Number: 2025930968

for Alana;
the taste of you burnt my mouth
with its sweetness

Contents

Introduction

Some time ago, as I sat in our annual back-to-school faculty meeting on the Friday before classes were due to start, a wise colleague stood up to speak. "My syllabi are written," he said, "but if the experience of past years is predictive, I'll spend the weekend anxiously fiddling with their language, in an effort to guarantee that the first day of classes on Monday goes perfectly." And then, gesturing ruefully out the window at the sun-soaked quad, he continued, "But the forecast for this weekend is gorgeous, and you all know how much I love to go mountain biking. If I were to put the question up for a vote, how many of you would encourage me to keep working on those syllabi? And how many of you would tell me to go mountain biking?" The chorus of catcalls and cheers was unanimous; we all wanted him to take the weekend off and enjoy the last days of summer. "Okay," he conceded, "you win. But here's my stipulation for you: everyone who encouraged me to take the weekend off and soak up the sun should do the same. Put away your laptops and try to have a bit of fun before the pressures and stresses of the semester begin in earnest." No one cheered this time, and if my reaction was any indication, my colleagues were much less enthusiastic about the prospect of abandoning their own work for the weekend. We all earnestly desired a carefree break for our colleague but felt queasy about taking time off ourselves.

As this anecdote suggests, pleasure is something we deeply desire for others but can be reticent to claim for ourselves. We want to provide the perfect gift at Christmas; we eagerly recommend the novels and television series we consume in a night; and we encourage our friend to have that piece of chocolate cake—she deserves it! Yet when our loved ones ask what we want for Christmas, many of us are quick to say, "I don't need anything." We regard the novels or TV series recommended by others warily, afraid we'll binge them and neglect other responsibilities. If we eat the cake at all, the piece that we dish for ourselves is often smaller than the one we would serve to a guest. Pleasure is an idea that we regard with misgiving, afraid that its allure might cause us to coast through life, abandoning ambition and duty.[1]

Even more than the general public, members of The Church of Jesus Christ of Latter-day Saints relate to pleasure with unease. We are the inheritors of a Christian tradition whose adherents have worn hair shirts and practiced self-flagellation to mortify the flesh because they believed that sensory enjoyment is deceptive, a worldly counterfeit for higher and holier feelings like joy. The Puritans and other Christians have often identified pleasure with temptation and with sexual appetites that must be constrained. But we know that pleasure is a gift from God, a capacity to appreciate sensation and beauty through physical bodies created in the image of our Heavenly Parents; when we hear a symphony or observe a sunset or savor a ripe

---

1. Charles Carver and other psychologists have actually theorized that the impulse to put one area of our lives in cruise control when we experience the pleasure of accomplishment is a helpful evolutionary adaptation. Our "first response to negative feelings is usually to try harder," Carver writes, but "when things are going better than they need to," the pleasure of success leads us to "ease back such that the subsequent rate of progress returns to the criterion" and we can redistribute effort to those areas of our lives in need of greater attention. See Charles S. Carver, "Pleasure as a Sign You Can Attend to Something Else: Placing Positive Feelings within a General Model of Affect," 248.

strawberry, we are experiencing pleasures that are essential components of the fulness of joy They intend for us. We experience pleasure when we caress the skin of a newborn as well as when a spouse's lips brush our own, and pleasure can be felt "in moments of creation, discovery, aesthetic contemplation, and helpfulness to others."[2] Pleasure is a conglomerate feeling prompted by a wide array of experiences, many of which are consistent with and even integral to our identity as children of God.[3] Before we can claim the divine inheritance for which this mortal experience is a necessary preparation, we must be reconciled to pleasure in its various manifestations and learn to respond to sensation appropriately.

---

2. Riane Eisler, *Sacred Pleasure: Sex, Myth, and the Politics of the Body*, 175. Eisler argues that pleasure, and especially sexual pleasure, was stigmatized by the medieval Christian Church in an effort to suppress "an earlier religious tradition that associated sexuality—as well as woman, and not just man—with the spiritual and the divine." The Bull God, whose coupling with the Goddess was an expression of worship imitated by her adherents, "became the horned and hoofed devil of Christian iconography. And sex, once a sacred gift of the Goddess—along with woman—became the source of all carnal evil." Eisler, 31.

3. The question of whether pleasure is unitary (a singular feeling prompted by many different experiences) or differentiated (several different feelings so closely linked to the experiences stimulating them that they cannot be regarded as the same thing) has prompted philosophical and scientific debate. With Immanuel Kant, I regard pleasure—whether generated by achievement, arousal, an appreciation of beauty, or any other cause—as a unitary phenomenon. For a consideration of the history and recent state of debate on this question, see Laurette Dubé and Jordan L. Le Bel, "The Content and Structure of Laypeople's Concept of Pleasure," 263–95.

The eagerness with which so many people encouraged my colleague to go mountain biking suggests that we already accept pleasure as a positive aspect of others' lives; our reservations about pleasure, then, are likely rooted in a suspicion of our personal capacity for self-regulation. In C. S. Lewis's beloved novel, *The Lion, The Witch, and the Wardrobe*, a young boy named Edmund takes one bite of an enchanted sweet and loses control of himself, "trying to shovel down as much Turkish Delight as he could," unaware that because of the spell placed upon this confection, "anyone who had once tasted it would want more and more of it, and would even, if they were allowed, go on eating it till they killed themselves."[4] Members of the Church have, perhaps, internalized the lesson of Lewis's novel too well. We wisely abstain from illegal drugs and habit-forming but legal substances like tobacco to avoid being ensnared by addictions; however, many Church members also practice a puritanic avoidance of seemingly innocent pleasures.

The journalist and religious critic H. L. Mencken bitingly characterized Puritanism as "the haunting fear that someone, somewhere, may be happy," but the anxiety suffered by contemporary Church members seems quite the opposite of Mencken's Puritanism.[5] We fervently hope that others elsewhere are happy while harboring the quiet worry that our own happiness is dangerous, uncertain as to whether our personal Christian practice is compatible with a genuine enjoyment of our embodied existence in the world. We want to comfort others and to mourn with them, to carry their burdens and accept their confidences. But we are reticent to receive comfort at their hands, and the idea of being comfortable or enjoying a pleasurable re-

4. C. S. Lewis, *The Lion, the Witch and the Wardrobe*, 37-38.
5. H. L. Mencken, *A Mencken Chrestomathy*, 624.

spite from those burdens can be anxiety-inducing. Why is it that the realization of our desires and the gratification of our senses scares us so much? What is it about pleasure that gives us pause?

* * * * *

When God spoke with Abraham, He covenanted to provide Terah's son with a posterity as numerous as the stars in the sky. On the first occasion that God promised to make Abraham "a great nation," he was already seventy-five years old (Gen. 12:2–4), and Isaac wouldn't be born for another quarter century (21:5).[6] The news that Sarah would, at long last, bear a child, must have been tremendously exciting for her. However, when three divine messengers visited the couple some years later, to reaffirm God's promise of posterity, Sarah listened to the declaration that she would give birth to a son with skepticism. And because it had "ceased to be with Sarah after the manner of women"— because she no longer menstruated and had gone through menopause—Sarah "laughed within herself, saying, After I am waxed old shall I have pleasure, my lord being old also?" (18:11–12). She likely felt incredulous, and perhaps an earlier bitterness at having been denied the opportunity to bear children was evident in her laugh and in the question that other translations render as, "Now that I am old and worn out, can I still enjoy sex?" or "Now that I am worn out and my husband is old, will I really know

---

6. Actually, God first makes this promise to Abram and, implicitly, Sarai. However, because the name change associated with the covenant in Genesis 17 is not directly relevant to my discussion of pleasure, I refer to the couple as Abraham and Sarah throughout, to avoid unnecessary complications for the reader.

such happiness?"[7] Notably, Sarah's question did not address what might have seemed like the main issue—the promise of posterity. Rather than ask, "Shall I have a son?" or "Shall I be fertile?" she asks whether she will be able to enjoy the prophesied blessing: "Shall I have pleasure?"

Her question is not about the Lord's ability to bring ovum and sperm together to create life but about His intent in doing so. After a lifetime of frustration, waiting, and wanting, she asks if the arrival of this promised child will simply be the means to a divine end, or if the conception and rearing of Isaac will be the blessing that she had long prayed for. Would the conception and delivery of the child she had desired, and then stopped expecting, be a source of pleasure in her old age or just a headache endured for the sake of fulfilling prophecy?

Although Sarah's question was posed in response to a specific promise from God, her query might be re-framed in more generally applicable terms. Does God intend that His children enjoy and take pleasure in mortality, or have we been sent to earth only to learn and grow through suffering and through the conflict that we all experience between bodily appetites and spiritual concerns? Such a question might be broken down into more specific inquiries: Does a loving Heavenly Father want us to delight in the food that we eat, or is He solely concerned with the nourishing and strengthening of our bodies? Does a loving

---

7. Unless otherwise indicated, all quotations of the Bible are from the King James Version of the Bible. The other translations quoted here are the Good News Translation and the Contemporary English Version of the Bible, respectively. Readers interested in a verse-by-verse comparison of these and many other English translations can access them on the Bible Hub website.

Heavenly Mother care whether we enjoy our journey, or is She solely concerned that we travel home in safety? Do loving Heavenly Parents want us to take pleasure in the sexual experience of procreation, or are They solely concerned with the mass production of bodies for Their spirit children?

The intuitively obvious answer to these questions is that God does care about our pleasure and enjoyment, and the teachings of prophets both ancient and modern support that conclusion. However, we often speak and behave in the Church as though our primary purpose on earth is to endure long enough and to pass through sufficient suffering to be exalted, postponing our own happiness, joy, and pleasure to a nebulous and distant postmortal experience. We hope that those we love take pleasure in the here and now but behave as though our personal enjoyments should be deferred.

Consider, again, the case of Sarah. Whatever excitement she might have felt at the prospect of becoming a mother, her anticipation of and belief in that pleasurable future clearly waned over time; after at least ten years of fruitless waiting, she gave up entirely. Convinced that the Lord had "restrained me from bearing," Sarah encouraged Abraham to take her enslaved servant Hagar as a second wife—a younger sexual partner who would give birth to the promised child on her behalf (Gen. 16:2–3). Even as she abandoned her dreams of sexual pleasure and the social status that would accompany her new position as a mother, Sarah clung to the belief that her husband was still worthy and capable of enjoying the process of conceiving and rearing children. Rather than pursue the promised blessing together, she encouraged Abraham to press forward alone. "You go on without me," she might have said. "I'll be fine here by myself."

Whether from personal experience or observation, all of us are familiar with the phenomenon of such self-abnegation in other, modern contexts: the friend who volunteers to stay behind when there aren't enough seats in the car or enough tickets for the event and the spouse who persists in cleaning or tax preparation or cooking as their companion heads for a couch. Encouraging others to enjoy life while we stoically endure boredom or work diligently in a support role might seem like a noble gesture of self-sacrifice, but the persistent deferral of our own pleasure for that of others inevitably breeds both resentment and a prideful humility rooted in smugness—a sense of superiority to those for whom we have sacrificed. Sarah discovered too late that unilateral sacrifice would breed bitterness: "My wrong be upon thee," she tells Abraham in a moment of self-righteous indignation (Gen. 16:5). Abandoning her own desires for the pleasures of motherhood and social status while encouraging Abraham to continue on in pursuit of a previously shared dream on his own was not the solution for which Sarah had hoped; although the generosity of her initial intent was laudable, it also proved unsustainable, and at some point she came to think "grudgingly" (Moro. 7:8) of Hagar and Abraham en- joying the pleasures she no longer felt capable of receiving.

Because happiness is a central purpose of human exis- tence, renouncing pleasure is a denial of our divinely de- signed human nature. Men and women were created "that they might have joy," the prophet Lehi taught (2 Ne. 2:25). And although we sometimes speak of joy in the Church as though it was a spiritual state separable from our em- bodiment, Restoration scriptures clearly indicate that joy is, at some level, contingent on our possession of a physical body and its various senses: "The elements are eternal, and spirit and element, inseparably connected, receive a fulness of joy; and when separated, man cannot receive a fulness of joy" (D&C 93:33–34). Joy is an embodied state, an experience combining spiritual and sensual stimuli.[8] To give up on pleasure and repudiate sensual enjoyment, then, is to disavow our own humanity and waste the embodied experience of desire that was designed for our benefit by loving Heavenly Parents.

The joy that Lehi spoke of encompasses the joy that Sarah sought: pleasure in conceiving and rearing children. But Lehi associates that joy with the state of Adam and Eve after the Fall, while Sarah connects it to their experience in paradise. In Genesis 18:12, when Sarah asks whether she shall, at last, have pleasure, the Hebrew word translated as *pleasure* in the King James Version of the Bible is a cognate

---

8. Elder Neal A. Maxwell has observed that "joy is obviously of a higher order than mere pleasure. Pleasure is perishable. It has a short shelf life. Mere pleasure is not lasting because it is constantly feeding on itself. Thus the appetites of the natural man, though frequently fed, are never filled. For instance, even as gluttony digests its latest glob, it begins anticipating its next meal. The same pattern prevails with regard to the praise of men, to lust, and to greed. Strange as it seems, so far as the carnal pleasures are concerned, the very act of their consumption insures the cancellation of their satisfactions. They just do not last!" To say that joy is "of a higher order than mere pleasure" is true in the same way that you might say bread is of a higher order than sugar. Bread is more substantial, more filling, more nutritious than sugar, and it leaves an eater full for far longer. But most bread recipes call for a pinch of sugar because bread tastes better and the yeast rises more effectively when a recipe involves sugar. You can eat bread without sugar, but the most delicious bread incorporates sugar just as a fulness of joy incorporates pleasure. See Neal A. Maxwell, "'Brim with Joy' (Alma 26:11).".

of the Hebrew word for *Eden*.[9] Readers of the original text would have understood that Sarah asked whether she could really, after all the difficulties and sorrows she had endured, return to the innocent and uncomplicated delights experienced by Adam and Eve before their Fall.

Imagining the experience of our first parents before their fateful encounter with fruit from the tree of the knowledge of good and evil, the poet John Milton considered their capacity for joy and pleasure in the absence of sin and shame. Lehi insists that the couple "would have had no children" in the garden, but whether or not their prelapsarian bodies were capable of conceiving children, Sarah—and Milton, after her—clearly envisioned a sexually active Adam and Eve (2 Ne. 2:23). Indeed, from Sarah's perspective, the sex enjoyed by Adam and Eve in the garden represented a pinnacle of pleasure, the standard to which she aspired. Milton describes their innocent conjugal attentions in his epic poem, *Paradise Lost*, where the pair

> Straight side by side were laid, nor turn'd I ween
> *Adam* from his fair Spouse, nor *Eve* the Rites
> Mysterious of connubial Love refus'd:
> Whatever Hypocrites austerely talk
> Of purity and place and innocence,
> Defaming as impure what God declares
> Pure, and commands to some, leaves free to all.
> Our Maker bids increase, who bids abstain
> But our Destroyer, foe to God and Man?
> Hail wedded Love, mysterious Law, true source
> Of human offspring, sole propriety
> In Paradise of all things common else.[10]

---

9. See Andrew R. Davis, "Eden Revisited: A Literary and Theological Reading of Genesis 18:12–13," 611–31.

10. John Milton, "Paradise Lost," IV. 741–52.

Anticipating the argument that sexual desire and "the Rites / Mysterious of connubial Love" are "impure" outgrowths of the Fall, Milton reminds his readers that God's commandment to multiply and "increase" predates the transgression of Adam and Eve. Wedded love and sexual intercourse are, as Sarah's question implies, Edenic pleasures to be enjoyed without guilt or embarrassment.

And yet, despite a theology that embraces the body as a source of spiritual power and joy; despite a theology that considers sexual intercourse, "the means by which mortal life is created[,] to be divinely appointed"; despite a theology that insists that "all spirit is matter" (D&C 131:7) and that there is no inherent sinfulness in the material or physical world, we remain suspicious of experiences that stimulate and delight the senses.[11] We seem to place more trust in Sigmund Freud and modern psychology than in the revelations received by Joseph Smith, associating our desire for pleasure with an unconscious and irrepressibly animalistic element of our psyche.[12] Modern prophetic teachings on

11. The First Presidency and Quorum of the Twelve Apostles of The Church of Jesus Christ of Latter-day Saints, "The Family: A Proclamation to the World."

12. Freud famously asserted that "in psychoanalytic theory we immediately assume that the course of mental events is automatically regulated by the pleasure principle. That is, we believe that the course of mental events is in every case given its impetus by an unpleasurable tension, and that it then goes in a direction such that its final state coincides with a reduction of this tension, i.e., with the avoidance of unpleasure or the production of pleasure." This automatic preference for pleasure was, in Freud's conception, a function of the id, that part of the mind in which instinct and biological imperatives are dominant, rather than rational thought. See Sigmund Freud, *Beyond the Pleasure Principle*, 51.

the topic tend to emphasize the dangers of the natural man and unbridled pleasure-seeking rather than the divinely-intended joys of embodiment. As a result, members of The Church of Jesus Christ of Latter-day Saints seeking an answer to Sarah's question in general conference addresses might reasonably conclude that pleasure must be avoided at all costs.

A keyword search or brief survey of sermons that touch on the topic could well give the mistaken impression that pleasure, like sin, must be eliminated from our lives entirely rather than embraced in moderation. Summarizing the findings of scientists discussing illegal narcotics, Elder M. Russell Ballard explained that "there is a mechanism in our brain called the pleasure center. When activated by certain drugs or behaviors, it overpowers the part of our brain that governs our willpower, judgment, logic, and morality. This leads the addict to abandon what he or she knows is right. And when that happens, the hook is set and Lucifer takes control. Satan knows how to exploit and ensnare us with artificial substances and behaviors of temporary pleasure."[13] Elder Richard G. Scott, for his part, warned that we "are here on earth for a divine purpose. It is not to be endlessly entertained or to be constantly in full pursuit of pleasure."[14] And Elder Neal A. Maxwell offered a reminder that "God's plan is not the plan of pleasure; it is the 'plan of happiness.'"[15] But these prophetic teachings are not condemnations of pleasure itself, so much as warnings against making it our highest priority. They remind us that pleasure is not the intended outcome of mortality and stress that enjoyment should not be an end, but an ancil-

---

13. M. Russell Ballard, "O that Cunning Plan of the Evil One."
14. Richard G. Scott, "Finding Joy in Life."
15. Neal A. Maxwell, "The Tugs and Pulls of the World."

lary outcome of actions taken for higher and holier reasons. As a closer examination of prophetic lives and teachings reveals, pleasure can be and often is an innocent byproduct of righteous living, as we seek the fulness of joy promised to the faithful.

Because pleasure is naturally enticing, prophets and apostles have more frequently warned against its prioritization than encouraged its pursuit.[16] The effect—although not, I believe, the intent—of these warnings has been to cultivate a widespread suspicion of pleasure. Notwithstanding our body-positive doctrine, which collapses the traditional Christian opposition between spirituality and materiality, we remain wary of our senses and anything that would gratify them. As a result, our sensory experience of mortality seems morally fraught: How can you delight in that first, buttery-sweet bite of a freshly baked cinnamon roll or fully appreciate the caress of a spouse if you suspect that these forms of pleasure conceal a hook with which Satan is attempting to reel you in like a trout? Yet the Church's Lion House Pantry sells cinnamon rolls whose sweetness is the caloric equivalent of a meal, and the Church consistently encourages sexual relations between those legally and law-

---

16. Perhaps the closest thing to an endorsement of pleasure in recent years is Elder Dieter F. Uchtdorf's declaration that "our beloved Father in Heaven wants all His children to have as much happiness as possible, so He has filled this world with beautiful, wholesome pleasures and delights, 'both to please the eye and . . . gladden the heart.' For me, flying brought great happiness. Others find it in music, in art, in hobbies, or in nature." But even this relatively enthusiastic endorsement of pleasure is offered as a contrast to "something more," besides which these pleasures pale, a "higher and more profound joy." See Dieter F. Uchtdorf, "A Higher Joy."

fully wedded according to God's law, though always in in-
direct language—e.g., "the means by which life is created."
In other words, pleasure is acceptable and even desirable in
some cases, even though it is dangerous and forbidden in
others. As Joseph Smith remarked in 1842, "That which is
wrong under one circumstance, may be, and often is, right
under another."[17] We have been well taught, by prophets
and apostles, about the circumstances in which seeking or
taking pleasure is wrong. But our education about how and
when and why to embrace pleasure, doing that which is
"right under another [circumstance]," has largely been left
to the media and other commercial or secular voices, of
which we are rightfully suspicious. Not enough has been
said about pleasure and its place in the plan of happiness.[18]

   Absent a clear understanding of the theological case for
pleasure, I and other Church members of my acquaintance
have naturally gravitated to an immoderate framework of
abstinence and indulgence, vacillating between denial and
gluttony. Neither extreme is pleasing to God. Monastic as-
ceticism and hedonistic gratification are, alike, perversions
of the temperate equanimity which our Heavenly Parents
have sent us to earth to acquire. Offering counsel to the
Philippians, the apostle Paul encouraged those early saints
to "rejoice in the Lord always: and again, I say, Rejoice. Let
your moderation be known unto all men. The Lord is at
hand. Be careful for nothing; but in every thing by prayer
and supplication with thanksgiving let your requests be
made known unto God" (Philip. 4:4–6). Joy and rejoicing,

17. Joseph Smith, *History, 1838–1856, Volume D-1*, Addenda, 3.

18. Not enough has been said about pleasure in contexts
outside of the Church either; James Russell has observed that
"pleasure is the most neglected topic in psychology." See James
A. Russell, "Introduction: The Return of Pleasure," 161.

he teaches, is a matter of mediation between the contrasting impulses of body and spirit. The saints of Philippi are to "be careful for nothing," or freely ask for that which they desire. And yet, Paul warns, prayers for the gratification of those desires should be counterbalanced by gratitude for and an acknowledgment of that which they have already received, so that thanksgiving acts as a check on their appetites. The goal is moderation: a relationship to pleasure and desire that acknowledges, integrates, and unifies the contrasting impulses of body and spirit so that we can learn the fulness of joy for which our souls were designed.

In the pages that follow, I attempt to unpack the doctrine of desire and pleasure as it has been revealed in the scriptures, through the example and teachings of the Savior Jesus Christ and those whom He has called to lead His church in different periods and places. My hope is that all who read will grow increasingly confident in their understanding of God's intent that we experience the pleasures of embodied joy here, in this life, while preparing for the fulness of joy awaiting us in the eternities. Eventually, we should each be able to answer affirmatively and with confidence the question Sarah posed to God's messenger: "Shall I have pleasure?"

1. The Creation and the Fall

Seven times, in the first chapter of Genesis, Elohim reflects upon the creation of celestial bodies and the earth and the various life forms that populate it. On each occasion, he declares that the resulting organization of bodies and life forms is "good" or "very good" (Gen. 1:4, 10, 12, 18, 21, 25, 31). In pausing to evaluate and appreciate the fruits of his labor, Elohim models the value of both work and pleasure; our earliest story about the world in which we live and the God whom we worship suggests that pleasure is an appropriate response to the environmental stimuli with which we are surrounded. Indeed, the second creation narrative in Genesis specifies that when Jehovah "planted a garden eastward in Eden," he caused "to grow every tree that is pleasant to the sight, and good for food" (2:8–9).[1] When Adam and Eve awoke in the garden, after the earth had been formed, divided, and beautified, they were surrounded by picturesque sights, the pleasing scent of blossoming flowers and trees, the gurgling murmur of flowing water, and a variety of delicious fruits, seeds, and

---

1. English translations of the first three chapters of Genesis obscure the fact that there are at least two divine beings participating in the Creation. In the original Hebrew, both Elohim and Jehovah contribute to the organization of the heavens, the earth, and its inhabitants, so in these sentences, I ascribe action to each of them. The King James Version generally translates Elohim as "God" (see Gen. 1:1–2:3) and Jehovah as "the LORD." Instances of "the Lord God" refer both to Jehovah and Elohim and occur only rarely outside the creation narrative in Genesis 2:4–3:24.

nuts.[2] In the beginning, we might say, God created pleasure, and it was good.

I appreciate C. S. Lewis's perspective on the divine origin of pleasure. In *The Screwtape Letters*, his demonic protagonist writes of the danger in steering human beings toward pleasure, which was created by the Enemy of Hell—God:

> Never forget that when we are dealing with any pleasure in its healthy and normal and satisfying form, we are, in a sense, on the Enemy's ground. I know we have won many a soul through pleasure. All the same, it is His invention, not ours. He made the pleasures: all our research so far has not enabled us to produce one. All we can do is to encourage the humans to take the pleasures which our Enemy has produced, at times, or in ways, or in degrees, which He has forbidden.[3]

The question, in other words, is not whether fruit found in the garden of Eden was meant to be delicious to the taste and very pleasurable—of course it was! The question is whether Adam and Eve were wrong to take pleasure in its fruits for some other reason—because they did so in the wrong way or at the wrong time or in the wrong degree.

Perhaps our anxiety about pleasure reflects a belief that the sensual stimuli provided by Elohim and Jehovah to Adam and Eve were too good, too tempting. After all, when Eve considered the fruit of the tree of the knowledge of good and evil, the Genesis account indicates that she rationalized its consumption at least in part because of the pleasure she anticipated it would provide. Because Eve "saw that the tree was good for food, and that it was pleasant

---

2. I recognize that Genesis names the first woman Eve after the Fall; however, in the interest of a more seamless reading experience, and because the issue of her naming isn't directly relevant to the topic at hand, I refer to her as Eve throughout.

3. C. S. Lewis, *The Screwtape Letters*, 44.

to the eyes, and a tree to be desired to make one wise, she took of the fruit thereof, and did eat" (Gen. 3:6). This verse might be considered an origin story for our uneasy relationship with pleasure. If Eve, in her innocence and amid the abundance of Eden's other delights, could not restrain her herself from gratifying a desire for pleasure (and wisdom), how can we hope that our fallen selves will cope with sensual stimuli in a more measured and appropriate manner? We regard pleasure with fear at least in part because of the Fall, and we worry that we might follow in Eve's footsteps, overcome by the promise of pleasure, only to find ourselves cast out of God's presence.

However, these paranoid readings of Eve's Fall as a cautionary tale warrant reconsideration on at least two grounds. First, the biblical text suggests that paranoia is itself a potential danger. When Jehovah first introduced Adam to the garden and instructed him not to eat of the forbidden fruit, lest he die, Eve was absent—as yet unformed. Her instruction about the tree of the knowledge of good and evil happens off camera, as it were, but by the time Eve confronts the serpent, she has clearly been told not to eat the fruit. Actually, her exchange with the serpent indicates that she had adopted additional, even more stringent beliefs about the fruit. When the serpent asks her about God's directive, Eve responds, "God hath said, Ye shall not eat of it, neither shall ye touch it, lest ye die" (Gen. 3:3). Whence the command not to touch the fruit? Elder Dallin H. Oaks reminds us that the Fall was a "planned offense" which "God had decreed." His purpose was not to prevent Adam and Eve from eating (much less touching) the fruit but to clarify that doing so "was formally prohibited" and would trigger a specified consequence: "Death hath passed upon all men, to fulfil the merciful plan of the great Creator" (2 Ne. 9:6).[4] Eve's inaccurate belief that touching would lead to death, then, came not from God but another, unknown source; perhaps it was a well-intentioned precautionary measure established by Adam to prevent even the appearance of disobedience to divine instructions. Whatever its source, the prohibition on touching functioned as a *chumra* or fence law exceeding the original commandment.[5] Considering the prohibition as a *chumra* and remembering Christ's teachings about the dangers of extralegal traditions helps to clarify why the paranoid imposition of restrictions above and beyond the law, no matter how well-intentioned, can be problematic.

Speaking to religious leaders about their excessive concern with handwashing, a requirement above and beyond what was required by the Law of Moses, Jesus condemned the accretion of false traditions because of their tendency to promote unintended negative consequences. What likely began as a well-intentioned desire to preserve the sanctity of offerings to God had become, in Jesus's day, a pretext for withholding wealth or goods from parents and others

---

4. Dallin H. Oaks, "The Great Plan of Happiness."

5. Interpretations of divine law that expand its scope are known as fence laws because of the instruction given in Deuteronomy 28:22: "When thou buildest a new house, then thou shalt make a battlement [a railing or fence] for thy roof, that thou bring not blood upon thine house, if any man fall from thence." Just as a new homeowner is directed to build a fence around the roof of their home to prevent unintentional physical injury to others, interpreters of the law establishing extralegal requirements or *chumrot* believed that they were preventing unintentional spiritual injury to others.

in need. The result, Jesus explained, was that promoters of *chumrot* had "made the commandment of God of none effect by your tradition" (Matt. 15:6).

Conducting a thought experiment about the potential consequences of enlarging God's original warning about the fruit into a tradition against touching it might illustrate the danger of converting prophetic warnings against specific forms of pleasure into a suspicion of pleasure writ large. Imagine, for example, that Eve is walking and sees something in the grass; bending down, she picks up a piece of fruit from the tree of the knowledge of good and evil before she realizes what it is. If God's original instruction not to eat the fruit was all she knew, she might shrug and throw it aside with no harm done. If, however, a well-intentioned Adam had told her that touching the fruit would cause death, she might—having safely handled the beautiful and delicious-smelling fruit—reasonably conclude that Adam was mistaken on both counts and that the fruit could be safely consumed. Forbidding that which is ancillary to danger and expanding the scope of that which is off-limits or taboo can lead us to question the necessity of abstaining from that which is actually dangerous. The Fall narrative of Genesis suggests that cultivating an atmosphere of paranoia and establishing fence laws around the commandments may inadvertently lead to the very outcomes we hope to prevent.

We can easily translate this lesson from Eve's Fall into more modern contexts. Parents would be wise to discuss the story of Corianton with their children, recounting the young man's fornication with "the harlot Isabel" and concluding with Alma's warning: "Know ye not, my son, that these things are an abomination in the sight of the Lord; yea, most abominable above all sins save it be the shedding of innocent blood or denying the Holy Ghost?" (Alma 39:3–5). To warn about the seriousness of sexual relations outside of marriage is a necessary parental duty (Mosiah 4:14–15), and sin of any sort should be shunned: "The Lord cannot look upon sin with the least degree of allowance" (D&C 1:31). But if parents fail to discuss what Alma means by "these things"—fornication openly committed by an ordained and publicly recognized representative of Jesus Christ—or actively imply that all sexual sins, from lustful thoughts and dirty talk to viewing pornography and masturbating, are equivalent to Corianton's sins, they have effectively told their children that touching the fruit will result in death. When, inevitably, such children experience a licentious thought or linger in curiosity and lust over a pornographic image to which they have been unintentionally exposed, they will expect the dire consequences promised to murderers and blasphemers; upon realizing, through sad experience, that not all forms of sexual sin are tantamount to murder, they might reasonably wonder whether fornication is really so terrible.

Sin itself must never be countenanced, but as King Benjamin warned his people, "there are divers ways and means [whereby we may commit sin], even so many that I cannot number them" (Mosiah 4:29). Browsing the internet may be a waste of time and may inadvertently expose us to pornography or other temptations, but it is not sinful in and of itself, so forbidding this or other simple pleasures only provides us practice in justifying prohibited (but non-sinful) behaviors. Better to be clear with Eve, and ourselves, by differentiating between transgression (eating the fruit) and that which is potentially problematic only because it might lead to transgression (touching the fruit). Building a fence around the law only invites sin and communicates a fundamental distrust of our capacity to choose, repent, and progress along the covenant path.

Progression, of course, is the second problem with reading Eve's decision to eat the fruit as a cautionary tale warning against pleasure. For the broader Christian world, the decisions of Eve and Adam to consume the forbidden fruit represent a catastrophic capitulation to appetite, whereby humanity collectively forfeited our innocence and immortality. But members of The Church of Jesus Christ of Latter-day Saints regard the Fall as a positive development both spiritually and physically—an extension of the work begun in creation, when the Lord beautified and gave variety to the face of the earth. The fruit and the Fall were the necessary means whereby humanity collectively progressed to the next stage of our growth toward godliness, as embodied agents capable of exercising faith when confronted with uncertainty and of choosing wisely amid the manifold pleasures and occupations of mortality.

Restoration scriptures provide a record of Adam and Eve celebrating in the aftermath of their progression from innocence to experience. Adam declared, "Blessed be the name of God, for because of my transgression my eyes are opened, and in this life I shall have joy, and again in the flesh I shall see God" (Moses 5:10). Eve similarly reflected, "Were it not for our transgression we never should have had seed, and never should have known good and evil, and the joy of our redemption, and the eternal life which God giveth unto all the obedient" (v. 11). It is impossible to both accept these celebratory remarks as scripture and condemn Eve's choice to eat the delicious fruit from what was apparently a beautiful tree. If the Fall was not problematic or regrettable, neither was Eve's appreciation of the pleasures associated with that experience. To treat the Fall

as a cautionary tale is to accept the broader Christian condemnation of Eve and abandon our faith in Restoration
endorsements of her wisdom.

Restoration scripture suggests that the Fall actually en-
hanced our ability to appreciate both sensual and spiritual
stimuli, to our benefit. We understand the experience of
Adam and Eve in the garden of Eden as a monochromatic
palette of joy and delight, but the Fall introduced a knowledge of evil—expanding, in figurative terms, the array of
colors with which they were familiar and heightening their
appreciation of the pleasures they had previously known.
Describing the utility and necessity of contrast, Lehi taught
his son Jacob "it must needs be, that there is an opposition in all things." In the absence of such opposition, Lehi
posited that we would experience "no life neither death,
nor corruption nor incorruption, happiness nor misery,
neither sense nor insensibility" (2 Ne. 2:11). We learn, in
mortality, by "sad experience," whether our own or that
of others, and make sense of our lives by comparing and
contrasting opposites: health and sickness, light and dark-
ness, pleasure and pain (D&C 121:39). As anyone who
has been sick quickly discovers, the joys of good health
can only be fully appreciated after we have experienced the
pains and inconveniences of illness; no one is more grateful
for the pleasures of a properly functioning body than an
individual recently recovered from injury or disease. The
contrast introduced by the Fall actually heightened Adam
and Eve's appreciation of both righteousness and pleasure
by exposing them to wickedness and pain.

Perhaps this, then, is the source of our anxiety—not
that pleasure led to Eve's transgression but that the Fall so
magnified our appreciation of sensual stimuli that we are
no longer able to resist its lure. Abinadi taught that the

Fall of Adam and Eve "was the cause of all mankind becoming carnal, sensual, devilish" (Mosiah 16:3), and Alma the Younger echoed that language, explaining that after the Fall humanity "had become carnal, sensual, and devilish" (Alma 42:10). That trio of adjectives associated with the Fall is curious. What does it mean to have become carnal or sensual? And why are those characteristics devilish? To say that we are carnal is simply to acknowledge that we are beings of flesh and bone, and our sensuality is a biological fact: We receive and process information about the world through our bodily senses.

When Abinadi and Alma taught that after the Fall human beings became carnal, sensual, and devilish beings, their warning had less to do with the nature of our physical bodies than our capacity to cope with spiritual death—our separation from the presence of Heavenly Parents. In Their immediate presence, we were able to consider the eternal implications of our individual choices; the majesty of divinity was immediately apparent, and we could always know, perfectly, what decisions would enable us to remain at or return to Their side. But after the Fall, Adam and Eve could have no direct knowledge of Heavenly Father's presence or His will. Instead, they had to rely on their bodily senses and mental faculties to understand the world around them and to guide their choices. To say that Adam and Eve became carnal and sensual after the Fall, then, is only to say that they exercised the rational faculties and sensory organs they had been given to understand the world in which they lived and to choose for themselves between bitter and sweet, pleasure and pain.

Since God created our bodies, neither adjective should be understood as inherently devilish; indeed, as Joseph Smith taught, the devil does not have a body and longs for one desperately. He craves corporeality and the integration of sense and spirit. And, the Prophet explained, our own God-given bodies represent a source of strength enabling us to resist Satan's temptations: "All Spirits that have bodies have power over those that have not hence men have power over Devils."[6] Embodiment is godly, not devilish, and our bodies—with the capacity to process the world through sensual stimuli—are sources of divine power. Our bodies should be reminders that we have already, in a premortal existence, resisted Satan's temptations, and sources of assurance that we are capable of rejecting his lies once again. Our fallen bodies are not liabilities in our effort to acquire divine attributes but the divinely given objects of devilish envy! There is nothing inherently evil or dangerous about our fallen, mortal flesh, our rationality, or our increased ability, after the Fall, to appreciate the pleasures of contrasting stimuli.

Prophets have repeatedly taught that we should exercise our mental and physical faculties to make wise decisions, so our identity as carnal and sensual beings can only be considered devilish if and when that divinely appointed decision-making process reflects satanic priorities. Chastising those who would seek to replace a rational and sensory-driven decision-making process with a quest for revelation in all things, President Dallin H. Oaks (then a justice of the Utah Supreme Court) shared this counsel with the students of Brigham Young University:

> [T]he Spirit of the Lord is not likely to give us revelations on matters that are trivial. I once heard a young woman in testimony meeting praise the spirituality of her husband, indicating that he submitted every question to the Lord.

---

6. Joseph Smith, "Discourse, 30 January 1842," 4. The same teaching is found in several other reports of the prophet's sermons.

She told how he accompanied her shopping and would not even choose between different brands of canned vegetables without making his selection a matter of prayer. That strikes me as improper. I believe the Lord expects us to use the intelligence and experience he has given us to make these kinds of choices.[7]

We must and should deploy the carnal, sensual faculties with which we have been endowed to make decisions; in this there is no sin, even though, as a result of our reliance on our eyes and ears and brains and hands, we will make mistakes.[8] Such errors are those of which Nephi spoke: "If I do err, even did they err of old; not that I would excuse myself because of other men, but because of the weakness which is in me, according to the flesh" (1 Ne. 19:6). Our dependence on sensory input and carnal rationality will necessarily lead to blunders and transgressions.[9] Such mistakes are a necessary, and even desirable, part of a mortal education that will facilitate our growth, learning, and development.[10] Decisions motivated by bodily appetites and sensory inputs only become sins when they are motivated by devilish pride.

7. Dallin H. Oaks, "Revelation."

8. See Dallin H. Oaks, "Sins and Mistakes."

9. On the fallibility of our senses, even when they are "functioning exactly right," and other reasons we are often mistaken, see Kathryn Schulz, *Being Wrong: Adventures in the Margin of Error*, 61.

10. As Elder Lynn G. Robbins reflected, "Hopefully, each mistake we make becomes a lesson in wisdom, turning stumbling blocks into stepping-stones. Nephi's unwavering faith helped him go from failure to failure until he finally obtained the brass plates," and God intends that our mistakes "shall give [us] experience, and shall be for [our] good." See Lynn G. Robbins, "Until Seventy Times Seven."

To act on carnal or sensual understandings of the world, in the pursuit of pleasure, is sinful only when an orientation toward pleasure is in conflict with the first and second commandments, to love God and to love our neighbor as ourselves; however, our removal from the presence of Heavenly Parents can make it more difficult to know how we should act on the imperfect sensory input that provides information about the world around us. Perhaps our clearest example of the conflict between carnal senses and the two great commandments is the biblical account of Eli's sons, Hophni and Phineas, who officiated in the temple at Shiloh. When men and women brought their offerings to the temple, these two would roast the slaughtered sacrifice for their own consumption "before they burnt the fat" (1 Sam. 2:15) reserved by law as God's portion: "All the fat is the Lord's" (Lev. 3:16). In other words, their decisions were driven by their tastebuds even when their desire for fatty meats came into direct conflict with divine imperatives to worship God and to serve the children of Israel. Enjoying fatty meats was not inherently sinful; if they had butchered their own sheep and roasted its flesh, they could have indulged their palates without neglecting their duty to God or neighbor. But the pride of Hophni and Phineas led them to seek their own pleasure at the expense of others. That pride, and not the pleasure of a well-marbled lamb shank, was the source of their sin, and our reliance on carnal and sensual information to make decisions is sinful only insofar as it entices us to similarly selfish actions.

Both the Creation and the Fall provided the human family with divinely orchestrated opportunities to experience pleasure. And as Eve's celebratory speech, offered in the wake of her transgression in the garden of Eden, suggests, pleasure can be and often is compatible with a love of God and neighbor. Her consumption of fruit from the tree of the knowledge of good and evil was consistent with a love of others, as it enabled Adam and Eve to have "seed," or children, and it also allowed them to better understand "the joy of redemption" provided by the Savior (Moses 5:11). Members of The Church of Jesus Christ of Latter-day Saints reject false traditions about the Fall that condemn Adam and Eve for overindulging carnal appetites. Their enjoyment of the delights provided in and out of Eden, by loving Heavenly Parents, was consistent with a divinely instilled desire to "be as gods," and nothing about the Fall or the bodies we enjoy because of the Fall should lead us to shun pleasure or to identify our desire for pleasure as sinful (Gen. 3:5). Our carnal and sensual faculties are intended to help us make decisions while separated from God's presence, and a desire for pleasure often points us toward divine imperatives, including the first commandment given to Adam and Eve, that they "multiply and replenish the earth" (Gen. 1:28). Acting on these instincts is only sinful when a self-centered, prideful pursuit of pleasure leads us to neglect the two great commandments identified by Jesus Christ; in this, as in all things, He is our Exemplar and Teacher.

2. The Life and Teachings of Jesus Christ

A study of the personal, embodied ministry of Jesus Christ provides a helpful perspective on pleasure. The biblical accounts of His retreat into the wilderness, following His baptism, make clear that the Son of God was willing and able to bridle His carnal appetites. The Gospel of Matthew records that "when he had fasted forty days and forty nights, he was afterward an hungered" (Matt. 4:2). Surely He hungered during the period of His fasting and not only after it had been completed, but Jesus persisted in prayer and solitude rather than seek out the pleasures of food and drink. This prolonged period of self-abnegation, in excess of that endurable by mortal men and women exposed to the elements, might be understood as part of His atoning mission, enabling Jesus to fulfill the words of Alma, who testified that the Christ would suffer "temptations of every kind" and "take upon him their infirmities, that his bowels may be filled with mercy, according to the flesh, that he may know according to the flesh how to succor his people according to their infirmities" (Alma 7:11–12). In His extreme hunger and thirst, the Savior felt a greater desire—and need—for food and drink than any we might know, even unto death. His refusal to break His fast and abandon preparations for His ministry is an example of abstinence and self-restraint that can comfort and strengthen us when it is necessary for us to forgo the pleasure of food and drink in obedience to God and service to our neighbor.

Lest we misconstrue this period of fasting as an effortless expression of the Son of God's divine nature, Matthew and Luke remind us that Jesus hungered—and the gospels also record that He was tempted by Satan. Following the prescribed period of His fast, when He was free to eat but had not yet returned from the wilderness, "the tempter came to him, [and] said, If thou be the Son of God, command that these stones be made bread" (Matt. 4:4). It would not have been a sin to eat, yet Jesus rejected this invitation, refusing to indulge His own appetites or salve His pride by working a miracle that would establish His divinity. Even though Jesus had miraculously provided food to others who were hungry in the desert during His premortal ministry to the Israelites as Jehovah, and even though He had already fulfilled the period of His fast, He deferred the pleasure of eating rather than exercise the keys of creation to satisfy a personal desire for food.

In resisting temptation, Jesus provided an example we can emulate when our own carnal desires and sensual inclinations tempt us to act in ways that trivialize our divine identity or to pursue pleasure for the sake of gratifying our pride. As C. S. Lewis has noted, only those who resist temptation fully appreciate its lure, and in His consecrated refusal to yield, Jesus gained an intimate and personal knowledge of the enticements He asks us to ignore.[1] No

---

1. Lewis memorably declared, "No man knows how bad he is till he has tried very hard to be good. A silly idea is current that good people do not know what temptation means. This is an obvious lie. Only those who try to resist temptation know how strong it is. After all, you find out the strength of the German army by fighting against it, not by giving in. You find out the strength of a wind by trying to walk against it, not by lying down. A man who gives in to temptation after five minutes simply does not know what it would have been like an hour later. That is why bad people, in one sense, know very little about badness. They have lived a sheltered life by always giving in. We never find out the strength of the evil impulse inside us until we try to fight it: and Christ, because He was the only man who never yielded

one better understands the desirability of pleasure—in
food and drink, in sexual relations, in opiates that distract
us from pain—than Jesus Christ, who rejected pleasurable
diversions from his redemptive mission so that He might
succor us in our hour of need.

And yet, the scriptural record plainly declares that Jesus
also succors us *through* pleasure, providing sensual delights
that afford us rest and relief from daily cares. Consider the
case of what John describes as the "beginning of miracles"
performed by Jesus (John 2:11). At a wedding feast attended by both Jesus and his mother, Mary, the supply
of wine was exhausted well before the end of the feast. At
Mary's entreaty, Jesus transformed water into wine, supplying all that was required for the feast to continue. This
much might be dismissed as an act of compassion for his
mother, irrelevant to the question of pleasure. But John
clarifies that the wine provided by Jesus was extraordinarily
delicious, such that the ruler of the feast remarked, "Every
man at the beginning doth set forth good wine; and when
men have well drunk, then that which is worse: but thou
hast kept the good wine until now" (John 2:10). Any wine
would have sufficed. All that Jesus needed to provide was a
wine of an equal or lesser savor to that which had already
been provided. But rather than meet some bare minimum
threshold, Jesus supplied refreshment of the highest quality, permitting those present at the feast to delight their
palettes and to take increased pleasure in the festivities.

The pleasurable gift offered at this "beginning of miracles" is reminiscent of the gifts given to Adam and Eve in
Eden and is consistent with Christ's actions throughout the
scriptural record. When the children of Israel were wander-

---

to temptation, is also the only man who knows to the full what
temptation means." See C. S. Lewis, *Mere Christianity*, 142.

ing the wilderness after their departure from Egypt, they complained that Moses and Jehovah had led them into a barren wasteland where they would starve. The premortal Christ responded as Jehovah by supplying them with manna in the morning and quail in the evening, and while He might have given them some blandly nutritious foodstuff (think of the chalky, flavorless protein bars marketed to athletes), the author of Exodus takes pains to emphasize how delicious this manna was. Each delicate, round flake of manna "was like coriander seed, white; and the taste of it was like wafers made with honey" (Ex. 16:31). Just as Jesus would later respond to His mother's request with the finest wine, unnecessarily gratifying guests at the wedding, so He responded to Israel's plea for food, as Jehovah, with a miraculously pleasurable comestible that exceeded the bare minimum caloric and nutritional requirements for maintaining life. He delights in giving good gifts to the human family, and the goodness of those gifts is often made manifest in the sensation of pleasure they provoke through touch, taste, hearing, sight, sound, or smell.

Jesus is the exemplary Giver of good and pleasurable gifts, but He also defended and modeled the reception of pleasure during His mortal ministry. In the same way that each of us must be willing to share a burden with others if the covenantal community is to fulfill our joint commitment to "bear one another's burdens," so each of us must be willing to receive pleasure, lest the good gifts of our bodies and of others' generosity be put to waste (Mosiah 18:8). Although the details of each account vary, all four of the Gospels portray a moment when Jesus is approached by a woman who anoints His body with costly, aromatic ointment. This was a moment that troubled those who observed it and that continues to challenge our understanding of His ministry today, but it was also important enough that Jesus commanded it be recorded and discussed, saying, "Wheresoever this gospel shall be preached throughout the whole world, this also that she hath done shall be spoken of" (Mark 14:9). All four of the evangelists took His directive seriously and included an account of His anointing, but my experience has been that Latter-day Saints and other Christians do not accord this event the serious consideration that Jesus asks us to give it. Each Gospel notes that one or more of those who observed this lavish and loving gesture objected, suggesting that Jesus should not have permitted the woman to proceed. But in all four accounts, Jesus defends the woman's actions, insisting that her expenditure of precious resources on a symbolic and pleasurable act was justified.

In the Gospels of Matthew and Mark, the woman anoints Jesus's head. Mark writes that she approached the Savior with "an alabaster box of ointment of spikenard very precious; and she brake the box, and poured it on his head" (Mark 14:3). Objecting that the ointment might, instead, have been sold and the proceeds given to the poor, several of Jesus's disciples complained, asking "Why was this waste of the ointment made?" (Mark 14:4). Their question characterizes any costly display of affection, grooming, or intimacy as a "waste," inappropriate for consecrated followers of Christ. They likely remembered the Master's earlier rebuke of a would-be-disciple who was challenged by Jesus to "sell whatsoever thou hast, and give to the poor" (Mark 10:21). They might reasonably have wondered why, if that man was required to forsake the material world and consecrate his goods to the poor, this woman should not have been required to do likewise. The explanation given by Jesus, that "she is come aforehand to anoint my body to the burying," has endowed the act with prophetic and theological significance and might suggest that her display of devotion and affection could properly be offered and received only in this particular instance because of His impending death (Mark 14:8). But Mark's account indicates that other motivations prompted both the woman's gift and the Savior's defense of her conduct.

Because the disciples seem so fixated on the expensive ointment, we naturally focus on it as well. However, the more symbolic element of the woman's worship is her breaking of the alabaster box in which the spikenard had been stored. She might have dipped a hand into the box and placed a drop on Christ's head, in the same manner elders today anoint the sick before administering a priesthood blessing. She might have opened her box and "poured" the contents on His head without destroying a vessel that was itself precious. Breaking the box was an act of extravagance that heightened the meaning of her gift by suggesting that no future use, whether as a decoration or storage container, could be more valuable than its sacrifice at this particular moment.

Her offering, which Jesus accepted and defended, was a more demonstrative gesture meant not only to prepare Jesus's body for burial but to fill his nostrils with the spicy and musky scent of spikenard, a scent that might have lingered throughout the imminent ordeal of Atonement and crucifixion as a comforting, sensory reminder of her love and appreciation. Through this gesture, as well as through the presence of female disciples at the foot of the cross, faithful women might have been symbolically present with Him throughout His suffering in a way that the male disciples who betrayed or slept or denied or simply left were not. Breaking the box meant that all of the ointment would be devoted to this singular purpose and that every strand of His hair would be coated in spikenard; when the Roman soldiers pressed a crown of thorns onto His head the next day and released a fresh wave of spikenard molecules into the air, He would have had reason to remember the pleasure of her gift at a moment otherwise exclusively devoted to pain.

Before Jesus offered a prophetic apology for her extravagance, He justified the woman's gift on other grounds. Chastising His complaining, parsimonious disciples, Jesus commanded, "Let her alone; why trouble ye her? she hath wrought a good work on me" (Mark 14:6). The Savior's first and most forceful defense was not an account of the unique circumstances that made this particular gesture proper or timely but a broader explanation that it is appropriate to give and receive pleasure as an expression of love. He graciously accepted the expensive perfume and her application of it to His head; given the quantity of ointment—enough to pour—Jesus likely also allowed the woman to rub it into His scalp and run her fingers through His hair. His receipt of this gift freely offered by another and His vigorous defense of such loving gestures, even when they consume resources that might otherwise be devoted to relieving the poor or other good and holy causes, should embolden us to receive the pleasures offered by Heavenly Parents and loving companions without being weighed down by guilt. The accounts in Mark and Matthew characterize gifts and pleasurable expressions of affection as "a good work" even when they might seem excessive or extravagant to outside observers.

In Luke and John, the woman washes and anoints Jesus's feet, rather than His head, using her hair to more uniformly distribute the costly ointment. This act was even more intimate than the reported anointing of Jesus's head and hair; it recalls the courtship of Boaz, when Ruth "came softly, and uncovered his feet, and laid her down" (Ruth 3:7). In John, the woman is identified as Mary, sister of Martha and Lazarus, but in Luke she is an anonymous "woman in the city, which was a sinner" and, readers have long conjectured, a prostitute whose touch outside observers of the day would have understood as inherently sexualized (Luke 7:37). In either case, the encounter would have been an intimately charged expression of physical affection and emotional attachment offered publicly and openly, so that "the house was filled with the odour of the ointment" (John 10:3). In both accounts Jesus receives the proffered gifts of ointment and physical touch with gratitude, defending the woman against her accusers.

In Luke's story of the sinful woman, the price of the alabaster box and the ointment is less significant than her bodily expressions of love for the Savior. Rebuking the Pharisee who had invited Him to dinner for his unspoken condemnation of the woman, Jesus "said unto Simon, Seest thou this woman? I entered into thine house, thou gavest me no water for my feet: but she hath washed my feet with tears, and wiped them with the hairs of her head. Thou gavest me no kiss: but this woman since the time I came in hath not ceased to kiss my feet" (Luke 7:44–45). The words of Jesus function as both a rebuke of Simon, who failed to express love through hospitable and pleasurable gestures, and an endorsement of the woman's actions. In His defense of the woman and of His own willingness to receive her, Jesus describes her intimate and pleasurable expressions of physical affection in redemptive terms: "Her sins, which are many, are forgiven; for she loved much" (Luke 7:47). Because the proffered pleasures—of cleanliness, of an aromatic unguent, of lips and hands and hair massaging His feet—are expressions of love, Jesus declares that the woman has been absolved of sin. Pleasure, in these particular circumstances, was not only acceptable but a conduit for interpersonal and divine grace.

There is no suggestion in Luke that this encounter immediately precedes the crucifixion or that the woman's actions symbolically prepare Jesus for burial; nevertheless, her pleasurable gift is still linked to the Savior's great atoning mission. To receive the pleasure proffered by another, this account intimates, is to allow that individual to fulfill their covenants through the expression of love. In caressing the Master's feet, she briefly bore His burdens, alleviating the aches and pains of an itinerant lifestyle. When she proffered the pleasures of physical touch and precious ointment, she produced the covenantal fruits Alma associates with baptism, and Jesus signaled His acceptance of her offering both by declaring that her sins were forgiven and, perhaps even more importantly, by receiving her gifts of touch and anointing. To reject pleasure, not because it is sinful but because it might be tenuously and tangentially linked to sin, as the touch of this woman was rejected by Simon, would have been to anticipatorily condemn the redeeming love of both the giver and the receiver in this exchange. In receiving the touch of a woman whose person Simon associated with sin, Jesus differentiated between act and intent; He showed that pleasures we, like Simon, might deem suspicious can also be gracious—the means of redemption.

Indeed, if we accept the account in John, Jesus not only received this gift but modeled its emulation. Mere days after Mary had anointed His feet and wiped them with her hair, while the scent of spikenard likely still lingered on His body, Jesus stripped to his smallclothes and began "to wash the disciples' feet, and to wipe them with the towel wherewith he was girded," as Mary had recently cared for

His own feet (John 13:5). Peter objected. The chief apostle might have been persuaded by Mary's example and the Savior's rebuke that it can be appropriate to give generously, but he was not yet convinced that it is appropriate or necessary to receive the pleasure and service offered by another. Peter's hesitance can be our own. Too often we misread the testimony of Paul, who taught the Ephesians "to remember the words of the Lord Jesus, how he said, It is more blessed to give than to receive," and conclude that it is blessed to give but selfish and wasteful to receive the freewill offerings extended by others (Acts 20:35). We have, as Riane Eisler writes, "been conditioned to associate pleasure with selfishness and insensitivity" and so refuse to receive the gifts others would willingly share with us.[2] Yet if we become so focused on giving and serving that we are unwilling to receive the kindness and pleasure offered by friends and family and strangers, we stand in the way of grace. Jesus washed at least twelve pairs of feet, but He also— when opportunity arose—allowed another to tend to His own feet. Whatever our natural inclinations, whether we are predisposed to indulgence or abstemiousness, we must find ways to participate on both sides of the equation, as both givers and recipients of pleasure, in imitation of Jesus.

If it seems that these four accounts of anointing and ointment and physical touch have been accorded disproportionate significance in the life of a teacher who disdained the world and its honors, consider the contrast that Jesus drew between Himself and John the Baptist. Immediately before the record of His anointing in Luke, Jesus observed that the critics of His day were dissatisfied with both the self-denial of John and His own compara-

---

2. Riane Eisler, *Sacred Pleasure: Sex, Myth, and the Politics of the Body*, 167.

tively lenient approach to questions of consumption: "For John the Baptist came neither eating bread nor drinking wine; and ye say, He hath a devil. The Son of man is come eating and drinking; and ye say, Behold a gluttonous man, and a winebibber, a friend of publicans and sinners! But wisdom is justified of all her children" (Luke 7:31–35). Jesus dismisses the accusation that He is gluttonous or a drunkard while acknowledging that He appreciates and consumes food and drink in a way that John did not.

Both the attendance of Jesus at dinner parties and John's more ascetic and solitary mode of life might be justified as wisdom, and His feasts reflect the same spirit as John's fasts.[3] Stories of Jesus feasting at banquets are so numerous in the Gospel of Luke that Robert Karris has observed, "In Luke's Gospel, Jesus is either going to a meal, at a meal, or coming from a meal."[4] Accounts, in all four Gospels, of the anointing of Jesus provide a unique perspective on His willingness to receive gifts and service from others, but it is a picture of His life and character that is in accordance with Luke's larger account of a teacher who endorsed the simple

---

3. As Matthew Croasmun and Miroslav Volf observe, "In Luke's gospel, many of Jesus' meals, his 'feasting,' have been in the mode of the 'true fast' of Isaiah 58. Taken together, the meals have been sites where Jesus has loosed the bonds of injustice, shared bread with the hungry, and welcomed the homeless poor into houses. And this climactic meal continues just this, inasmuch as Jesus' disciples themselves are rich and poor, sinners all, called to the good news of Jubilee: forgiveness of sins, of debts, and an invitation to be at home at the feast of the kingdom of God. Throughout Luke, Isaiah's true *fast* is enacted in the *feasting* of Jesus and his followers." Matthew Croasmun and Miroslav Volf, *The Hunger for Home: Food & Meals in the Gospel of Luke*, 85.

4. Robert J. Karris, *Eating Your Way Through Luke's Gospel*, 14.

pleasures of life—a meal with friends, reclining at the table, and footcare after a day spent walking.

Not only was Jesus Himself a frequent celebrant at meals and banquets, but His teachings and parables also revolved around the pleasures of feasting and celebration. In His parable of the prodigal son, for example, Jesus describes a young man who "took his journey into a far country, and there wasted his substance with riotous living" (Luke 15:13). This prodigal's search for pleasure carries him far from home and is excessive, a waste of the inheritance with which he was invested by his father. But when he comes to himself and returns to his father in humility, seeking only to be "as one of thy hired servants," the father responds by throwing a party (v. 19). He instructs servants to bring "the best robe, and put it on him; and put a ring on his hand, and shoes on his feet: and bring hither the fatted calf, and kill it; and let us eat, and be merry" (vv. 22–23). Although a love of pleasure and dissipation might be construed as the reason for his reduction to poverty, the father's response is not to shield his son from fine food and drink and clothes but to welcome him home with a banquet and music and dancing. In response, the prodigal's older brother refuses to participate in the festivities, complaining to the father that, despite his diligent labors, "thou never gavest me a kid, that I might make merry with my friends: but as soon as this thy son was come, which hath devoured thy living with harlots, thou hast killed for him the fatted calf" (vv. 29–30). The older brother objects to the music and the dancing and the fine clothes and the rich food, particularly because he has never sought pleasure for himself and because a pursuit of pleasure represents all that he despises in the younger son. Yet the father insists, "It was meet that we should make merry, and be glad" (v. 32). In His teachings, as well as in His lived experience, the Savior defended pleasure against the censures of the self-righteous.

Centuries of commentary, and the popular title ascribed to this story, invite us to poor or partial readings of the parable. Introducing the story, Jesus declares, "A certain man had two sons," and yet we commonly refer to this as the parable of the prodigal son—ignoring or effacing the existence of a second son (Luke 15:11).[5] A better title would be the parable of the two sons, or, more descriptively, the parable of the prodigal son and the abstemious son, the prodigal son and the puritanical son. We readily recognize the nature of the prodigal's error; he cared too much for pleasure and sought it at the expense of all else, until he was impoverished and estranged from all who loved him. When wise commentators redirect our attention to the elder son, they often characterize his failure as envy or pride. Elder Jeffrey R. Holland, for example, said of this older son that, "he has, as yet been unable to break out of the prison of himself. He is haunted by the green-eyed monster of jealousy."[6] The older brother *is* envious, as Sarah came to be envious of Hagar, but envy is not the older brother's defining characteristic. Both the parable's opening and its action

---

5. As Amy-Jill Levine argues, "Jesus's Jewish audience would be reminded of other men and their two sons: Cain and Abel, the sons of Adam; Ishmael and Isaac, the sons of Abraham; Jacob and Esau, the sons of Isaac; and so on." The title traditionally given to this parable obscures those allusive associations because "how we identify this parable already determines how we understand it." See Amy-Jill Levine, *Short Stories by Jesus: The Enigmatic Parables of a Controversial Rabbi*, 10, 242.

6. Jeffrey R. Holland, "The Other Prodigal."

indicates that the brothers are, in literary terms, foils: they represent opposed values.

Readers recognizing that the younger son is a spend-thrift who "wasted his substance" should also recognize that the older son is a skinflint who never allowed himself or others to enjoy the fruits of their labor. Each is prone to extreme behavior and represents one half of the dual temptations memorialized by William Shakespeare: "Thus do I pine and surfeit day by day, / Or gluttoning on all, or all away."[7] While the younger brother indulges in a surfeit of pleasure, the older brother lives in a state of repression and self-denial—"all away"—even as he pines and yearns for a taste of the good life he sees the younger son enjoying. To call this story the parable of the prodigal son is to ignore the older son's extreme and dangerous suppression of the desires that the younger brother too freely gratifies before making his penitent return to a delighted father.

The older brother is a diligent worker and obedient son, but he is also a self-made martyr unwilling to acknowledge or take responsibility for his own desires. When the father invites him to celebrate his younger brother's return, the older son complains, "Lo, these many years do I serve thee, neither transgressed I at any time thy commandment: and yet thou never gavest me a kid, that I might make merry with my friends" (Luke 15:29). In blaming his father, this older son throws the onus for his own joyless life onto an-other. Though he knows, from experience, that the father granted his young brother's extravagant request for his inheritance—half the estate, even before their father had passed—the older son never voiced his own more modest desires or asked the father for permission to slaughter a goat

---

7. William Shakespeare, "Sonnet 75," *The Complete Works of Shakespeare*, 1728.

and hold a banquet for his friends. The older son blames his father for the frustrated, pent-up life he's lived, but the father reminds his firstborn that "all that I have is thine" (v. 31). This declaration of joint stewardship might strike the reader as a belated revelation that the older son should have been informed of sooner. But it is a reminder, not a revelation; when the prodigal asks for his inheritance, the father "divided unto them his living" (v. 12). In other words, both the puritanical older son and the prodigal younger son— *them*—were given a portion of the father's property at the same time.[8] The older son had always known he was free to slaughter a kid and make merry with his friends, but he never acted on those impulses. He preferred to hold a grudge against his father and to view himself as a virtuous victim rather than enjoy a modest pleasure and lose track of the bright line that distinguished his self-denying identity from his brother's self-indulgent identity.

The older son's behavior recalls President Dieter F. Uchtdorf's allegory of the cruise ship. He describes a man eager to sail the Mediterranean Sea and visit the cities of Rome, Athens, and Istanbul who

---

8. In this respect the elder son is, appropriately, like Jesus Christ, who testified that "all things that the Father hath are mine" (John 16:15). But unlike the elder son, Jesus never abdicates his agency or suggests that the Father has somehow constrained his desires. In the garden of Gethsemane, he prays, "Abba, Father, all things are possible unto thee; take away this cup from me," but where the elder son of his parable might complain that the father left him no choice but to suffer, Jesus concludes in humility, "nevertheless not what I will, but what thou wilt" (Mark 14:36). The elder son outwardly complies with what he believes to be the father's will, but he complies resentfully, with his unfulfilled and repressed desires festering within.

saved every penny until he had enough for his passage. Since money was tight, he brought an extra suitcase filled with cans of beans, boxes of crackers, and bags of powdered lemonade, and that is what he lived on every day.

He would have loved to take part in the many activities offered on the ship—working out in the gym, playing miniature golf, and swimming in the pool. He envied those who went to movies, shows, and cultural presentations. And, oh, how he yearned for only a taste of the amazing food he saw on the ship—every meal appeared to be a feast! But the man wanted to spend so very little money that he didn't participate in any of these. He was able to see the cities he had longed to visit, but for the most part of the journey, he stayed in his cabin and ate only his humble food.

On the last day of the cruise, a crew member asked him which of the farewell parties he would be attending. It was then that the man learned that not only the farewell party but almost everything on board the cruise ship—the food, the entertainment, all the activities—had been included in the price of his ticket. Too late the man realized that he had been living far beneath his privileges.[9]

Like the parable of the two sons, President Uchtdorf's story clearly suggests that we might mistakenly pass through mortality without enjoying all that the Father has given us, including the pleasures of food and drink and not only the more refined or intellectual appreciations of passing through the world's great cities and learning of their histories and cultures. Both stories warn that a fear of pleasure—that it might cost too much; that it might overwhelm our senses; that it might lead to a debauched life of riotous living—might lead us to reject or misuse our rightful inheritance.

---

9. Dieter F. Uchtdorf, "Your Potential, Your Privilege."

The younger son's prodigality is clearly condemned by the parable and so, I would argue, is the older son's immoderate suppression of appetite and pleasure. They represent contrasting extremes we should shun while striving for a more temperate middle ground. Better for the younger son if he had exercised a modicum of self-restraint; better for the older son if he had made space in his life for modest pleasures and resisted the siren song of martyrdom. Alma repeatedly exhorted that we should be "temperate in all things" (Alma 7:23, 38:10), and Paul similarly taught, "every man that striveth for the mastery is temperate in all things" (1 Cor. 9:25). Both sons stray from the ideal of temperance and moderation. Their contrasting examples of excess should caution us equally against extremes of indulgence and extremes of suppression.

The Savior's parable of the prodigal and puritanical sons, like His life, suggests a need for moderation in our relationship to desire and pleasure. He fasted for forty days in the wilderness and demonstrated his capacity for self-denial in the service of a higher cause. Yet when His mother asked for wine, Jesus provided a vintage of the highest quality, and when He was invited to feast in the company of sinners, Jesus gracefully accepted the pleasures offered Him, whether the kisses and caresses of a woman seeking forgiveness or the extravagant application of precious, perfumed ointment to His head and feet. Both in His ability to forgo pleasures when they would distract Him from the higher mission to which He had been called and in His ready willingness to receive, enjoy, and share the pleasures of this mortal creation, Jesus is our Exemplar. His teachings, as well as His life, are reminders that "to every thing there is a season, and a time to every purpose under the heaven": a time to feast and a time to fast; a time to break the alabaster box of precious ointment and a time to forego its use so that the proceeds might be sold for the poor; a time to embrace and a time to refrain from embracing; a time to kill the kid and make merry with your friends; and a time to refrain from riotous living (Eccl. 3:1).

3. Safety and Risk

Although we sometimes pay lip service to the truth that there is a time and season for enjoying each of the various pleasures enumerated in Ecclesiastes, members of The Church of Jesus Christ of Latter-day Saints have also tacitly agreed that some pleasures are more acceptable and less dangerous than others.[1] Certain styles of music, for instance, are endorsed without reservation, while some genres are deemed appropriate only in specific times and locations, and still other forms of music are rejected entirely. In more general terms, we are inclined to identify some categories of pleasure as safe and others as risky.

This approach to pleasure mimics the risk-assessment methodology Paul Slovic describes as "intuitive toxicology."[2] Toxicologists know that the dose makes the poison; even water might be lethal if we consume enough of it, while our bodies are quite capable of processing deadly poisons in appropriately small doses—the amount of arsenic contained in an apple seed, for instance, poses little risk to our health. But the layperson treats water as if it were harmless

---

1. In so doing, we trail in the wake of both traditional Christian thinking regarding the Fall and the philosophical influence of John Stuart Mill's utilitarian logic regarding "higher and lower pleasures," which was predicated on the view that matter and the body are corrupt and inferior to mind or spirit. Elizabeth Anderson explains that Mill believed we "rank the pleasures of certain faculties higher than the pleasures of others because they judge the former to be more dignified." See Elizabeth S. Anderson, "John Stuart Mill and Experiments in Living," 11.

2. See Nancy Kraus, Torbjörn Malmfors, and Paul Slovic, "Intuitive Toxicology: Expert and Lay Judgments of Chemical Risks," 285–315.

and considers any exposure to arsenic a health crisis. With our pleasures, as with our poisons, the dosage is a critical but largely disregarded factor. Latter-day Saints broadly endorse exercising, reading the "best books," spending time in nature, and viewing art as unproblematic pleasures to be enjoyed without constraint, but they are also likely to express suspicion of desserts and sex and movies or television as potentially hazardous pleasures to be enjoyed infrequently or with caution (D&C 88:118). These distinctions between aesthetic and physiological and cognitive pleasures frequently represent arbitrary cultural preferences rather than doctrinal and moral differences; our predilections and categorizations are often imprecise and inherited, not a matter of revealed truth.[3] We assess our pleasures like our

---

3. As Laurette Dubé and Jordan L. Le Bel observe, there have been various attempts to identify subcategories of pleasure, which we are still influenced by today. Greek philosophers such as Plato, Aristotle, and Epicurus differentiated between pleasures of the body and pleasures of the soul. The influential eighteenth-century English philosopher Jeremy Bentham proposed fourteen different categories of pleasure. More recent proposals include those of "Duncker (1941) [who] sidestepped the body-soul dichotomy and proposed three types of pleasure: *sensory pleasures*, for which the immediate object of pleasure is the nature of a sensation (e.g., the flavour of the wine, the feel of silk); *aesthetic pleasures*, derived from sensations expressive of something, offered by nature, or created by man (e.g., sunsets, music); *accomplishment pleasures* represent the emotional, pleasant consciousness that something valued has come about (e.g., mastery of a skill, sport performance)," and "Tiger (1992) who identified four pleasure types: *physio*-pleasures (sensations or physical impressions obtained from eating, drinking, lying in the sun), *socio*-pleasures (borne of the company of others), *psycho*-pleasures (satisfaction from individually motivated

poisons: intuitively, without a careful examination of the data or the doctrine.

Because our embodied souls process these varied pleasures in distinctive ways—looking at a painting activates one set of neural pathways while viewing a movie activates another—there is wisdom in differentiating between various sources of pleasure. But our instinctive sorting of "safe" and "risky" pleasures obscures the similarities in these activities—exercise and sex, for example, release the same mood-boosting endorphins into our bloodstream—that have led individuals to overindulge in pleasures we instinctively identify as safe. Rather than relying on an intuitive and unspoken, culturally driven risky-safe binary, we would be better served by asking whether our participation in various pleasurable activities is motivated by an appreciation for the Creation that draws us into loving relation with God and others or by selfishness and a desire to escape the pain of our perceived separation from God and others.

The shifting moral valence of a specific pleasurable activity becomes evident when we examine the evolution of cultural attitudes toward that activity over the course of years, decades, and centuries. Because of its contemporary association with classical music and formal attire, the waltz is today considered a fairly conservative form of dance that might appropriately be practiced by anyone, without fear of impropriety or undue temptation. However, when it first became popular in the eighteenth and nineteenth centuries, the waltz was sometimes described as a "forbidden dance" because of the close proximity in which partners

---

tasks or acts), and *ideo*-pleasures (borne of ideas, images, and emotions privately experienced)." See Laurette Dubé and Jordan L. Le Bel, "The Content and Structure of Laypeople's Concept of Pleasure," 265–66.

spun and twirled around the dance floor.[4] The Church sponsors Brigham Young University's ballroom dance team and thus endorses the waltz, at least implicitly, but such a position or partnership would have been deemed scandalous in previous centuries.[5] In the present moment, I can hardly imagine the formation of a BYU twerking team, given the sexualization of and racial animus against that particular style of dance, but it may eventually—like the waltz—be deemed a relatively conservative form of cultural expression. Which pleasures are deemed dangerous and which are socially and ecclesiastically acceptable is a standard that can fluctuate over the course of generations.

If the moral import of a particular style of dance is contingent on cultural context, it is also contingent on the personal perspective and past experience of the participants. When my wife, Alana, and I attended the ballet recently, we both anticipated an innocent evening of graceful movement in celebration of the human body. Alana's enjoyment of the performance was uncomplicated; she felt uplifted and edified by the dancers. However, my experience was quite different. Because of my academic training in the history of sexuality, I recognized a number of signals during

---

4. See, for example, Mademoiselle Laloine's intimation "that the waltz was a forbidden dance to young ladies" in Catherine Gore, *Fascination, and Other Tales*, 305.

5. Indeed, in the early twentieth century, Church leaders instructed young women that the waltz, or "round dancing, is often indecent and immodest, and is even more dangerous, physically, than the plain 'square' dance or quadrille." See "Lesson VI: Ball Room Etiquette," 46. I am grateful to Ardis Parshall, who first brought this source to my attention in her transcription of the *Young Woman's Journal*; see Ardis E. Parshall, "Proprieties and Usages of Good Society—Lesson VI. Ball Room Etiquette."

the final number in both costuming and lyrics that led me
to believe the piece was a celebration of transgressive and
violent sexual attitudes and practices. As a result, what was
an inoffensive pleasure to Alana represented a morally re-
pugnant performance to me.

Evaluating the morality of sensory experiences, then,
cannot be accomplished with a one-size-fits-all rubric; the
attitudes and experiences we bring to our participation in
pleasurable activities will help determine whether they are
appropriate or problematic. As Jesus taught, it is "not that
which goeth into the mouth [that] defileth a man; but that
which cometh out of the mouth" (Matt. 15:11). Because of
our widely varying experiences, attitudes, intentions, and
perspectives, the same form of pleasure that seems innocent to some might be recognized as pernicious by others.
Broader cultural shifts, such as the transition of the waltz
from forbidden to respectable, occur as many individuals adopt new attitudes about the meaning of a particular experience—even when the nature of that experience
may not change.[6] The meaning of a particular pleasure is

----

6. Sometimes our shifting perception of a particular pleasure
is not the result of external cultural shifts but of a psychological
phenomenon characterized as the hedonic treadmill. Because
novelty often contributes to pleasure, many people enjoy the
second iteration of an experience less than the first. Your second
bite of cake, your second kiss, your second viewing of a Broadway
show is likely to be less pleasurable and impactful than the first.
Even permanent changes—such as winning the lottery—are
subject to this effect; the first minute in which you have won
the lottery is likely to be ecstatic, but by the end of the first
month, it is likely that your happiness will return to something
like the baseline level established prior to winning the lottery,
and you will again be disgruntled at minor life events, such as a

contingent, at least in part, on what "cometh out of" our mouths, bodies, and minds in response to external stimuli and to cultural values that shift over time.

A better example of the contingent nature of pleasure—because of the clear connection to leaders and teachings of The Church of Jesus Christ of Latter-day Saints in its semi-annual general conference—might be the widespread acceptance, within the Church, of William Shakespeare's plays as quasi-canonical standards of truth, beauty, and virtue. Over fifty years of general conference, between 1971 and 2020, the plays and poems and person of Shakespeare were cited by speakers in general conference more than sixty times; every year, listeners could expect to hear one or more speakers present the Bard of Avon's work as a source of sacred wisdom illustrating divine truth. Leaders and members of the Church have revered Shakespeare in the same way that Betty Smith honored him in her classic novel *A Tree Grows in Brooklyn*, where every night, "before they went to bed, Francie and Neeley had to read a page of the Bible and a page of Shakespeare."[7] The excellence of Shakespeare is widely recognized both in and out of the Church, but the pleasure afforded by his plays and poems is hardly so unproblematic as our collective embrace of his words might suggest.

During Shakespeare's lifetime, the playhouse was widely understood by conservative religious leaders in England to be a den of iniquity. Because female roles in sixteenth- and seventeenth-century English theaters were played by boys and men in women's attire, the playhouse was condemned by clergymen as a setting that promoted sodomy and other

---

slowdown in traffic. For further discussion of this phenomenon, see Daniel Kahneman, "Objective Happiness," 3–25.

7. Betty Smith, *A Tree Grows in Brooklyn*, 51.

forms of illicit sexual indulgence. In his account of the early modern English theater, Bill Bryson recounts the story of a young wife who

> pleads with her husband to be allowed to attend a popular play. Reluctantly the husband consents, but with the strict proviso that she be vigilant for thieves and keep her purse buried deep within her petticoats. Upon her return home, the wife bursts into tears and confesses that the purse has been stolen. The husband is naturally astounded. Did his wife not feel a hand probing beneath her dress? Oh, yes, she responds candidly, she had felt a neighbor's hand there— "but I did not think he had come for *that*."[8]

Plays now celebrated by Church leaders from the pulpit were once identified as transgressive forms of entertainment that promoted sodomy, gender confusion, and licentiousness—against which religious leaders contemporary with Shakespeare railed in Sunday sermons.

But perhaps, a reader might object, reading the plays rather than watching them performed in their original, early modern context renders them inoffensive. It is true, to a point, that Shakespeare's most transgressive and troubling scenes can be more easily stomached on the page than the stage: far easier to read about the rape and dismembering of Lavinia in *Titus Andronicus* than see the bloody stumps where her hands used to be and hear her tortured, tongueless voice. Yet, the language of Shakespeare's work in *Hamlet* (the play most frequently quoted in general conference) and other canonical texts is still saturated with sexual, and sometimes raunchy, jokes, as many, many commentators have noted. It was not merely the playhouse that promoted extra-marital sex and other actions and attitudes

---

8. Bill Bryson, *Shakespeare: The World as Stage*, 73.

at odds with Church teachings but Shakespeare's words in the plays themselves.

My aim in highlighting the violent and sexual content of Shakespeare's plays is not to argue that the works are morally suspect or that they should no longer be quoted in general conference lest the Church and its leaders be tainted by association. The biblical book of Judges is, frankly, more offensive than anything dreamed up by Shakespeare. Instead, I want to suggest that neither *Hamlet* and other "best books," nor exercise, nor an appreciation of the natural world are the safe, wholly unproblematic sources of inspiration and pleasure we sometimes treat them as. I have known men and women whose excessive interest in exercise eventually led them to distance themselves from God and others whose devotion to nature came to supersede their commitment to baptismal covenants. Every pleasure is an Eden, an inflection point where we communicate, through appetite, our alignment with or rejection of God. And just as in the original garden, our growth and progression is predicated not on the restriction of our appetites to "safe" pleasures but on an ability to consecrate our enjoyment of every pleasure compatible with our identity as children of God, even and perhaps especially those pleasures that might be culturally designated as dangerous.[9] Our purpose

---

9. "Perhaps especially" because in our media-saturated world it can seem difficult or even impossible to identify safe havens of rest and wholesome recreation where we can be sure that no unholy language or practice will intrude upon our enjoyment of one another and the creation. So much more important, then, to be able to consecrate pleasurable experiences in an environment of competing values and voices, rather than deferring pleasure endlessly until we've been ensconced behind figurative (or literal!) monastery walls.

in mortality is to align our wills with the will of God; having done so, we will learn the truth of Hamlet's words, that there is danger neither in dessert nor in Denmark, in sex nor in Shakespeare, "for there is nothing either good or bad, but thinking makes it so."[10]

Our relationship with pleasure would be much improved if we followed the example of President Russell M. Nelson and left behind the naïveté of good-bad binary thinking to embrace a more nuanced consideration of how particular pleasures enhance or inhibit our love for God, for His creation, and for others. In describing the matu-

---

10. Shakespeare, *Hamlet*, *The Complete Works of Shakespeare*, 1114. As Paul says, "One man esteemeth one day above another: another esteemeth every day alike. Let every man be fully persuaded in his own mind. He that regardeth the day, regardeth it unto the Lord; and he that regardeth not the day, to the Lord he doth not regard it. He that eateth, eateth to the Lord, for he giveth God thanks; and he that eateth not, to the Lord he eateth not, and giveth God thanks" (Rom. 14:5–6). The key consideration, in Paul's estimation, is not the action but what we understand the action to communicate about our commitment to God. Yale psychologist Paul Bloom likewise considers our belief about pleasurable experiences, rather than the nature of those experiences, to be the factor that most determines how we conceive of them: "People insist that the pleasure they get from wine is due to its taste and smell, or that music is pleasurable because of its sound, or that a movie is worth watching because of what's on the screen. And of course this is all true . . . but only partially true. In each of these cases, the pleasure is affected by deeper factors, including what each person thinks about the true essence of what he or she is getting pleasure from." See Paul Bloom, *How Pleasure Works: The New Science of Why We Like What We Like*, 24.

ration of his thinking about the Sabbath day, President
Nelson explained:

> In my much younger years, I studied the work of others who
> had compiled lists of things to do and things *not* to do on
> the Sabbath. It wasn't until years later that I learned from the
> scriptures that my conduct and my attitude on the Sabbath
> constituted a *sign* between me and my Heavenly Father.
> With that understanding, I no longer needed lists of dos
> and don'ts. When I had to make a decision whether or not
> an activity was appropriate for the Sabbath, I simply asked
> myself, "What *sign* do I want to give to God?" That question
> made my choices about the Sabbath day crystal clear.[11]

This shift helped President Nelson to exercise his agency—
the first gift of God—more meaningfully. Instead of relying
on the opinions of others, who had identified actions appropriate for and inappropriate for the Sabbath day, he made
his own decisions about whether an activity would communicate his love of and reverence for God or the opposite.

Significantly, this approach places less emphasis on *what*
the activity is and much more emphasis on *why* we are en-
gaging in that activity. To paraphrase a well-known line of
discussion about Sabbath day observance, the Lord cares
less about whether we are working with an ox in the mire
on the Sabbath day than about whether we pushed it into
the mire on the previous night. So, too, in our relationship
to pleasure. Rather than locating a particular pleasurable
experience on lists of approved or forbidden activities, our
evaluation of whether it is an appropriate use of time and
other resources should begin with motive—the question of
why we might engage in it.

When the Lord declared to Joseph Smith that He had
created this earth for the pleasure and benefit of the hu-

---

11. Russell M. Nelson, "The Sabbath Is a Delight."

man family, He also stipulated that He would evaluate our use of this gift by considering our motives. Following a discussion on fasting and food preparation, the Lord explained that

> inasmuch as ye do these things with thanksgiving, with cheerful hearts and countenances, not with much laughter, for this is sin, but with a glad heart and a cheerful countenance—Verily I say, that inasmuch as ye do this, the fulness of the earth is yours, the beasts of the field and the fowls of the air, and that which climbeth upon the trees and walketh upon the earth; Yea, and the herb, and the good things which come of the earth, whether for food or for raiment, or for houses, or for barns, or for orchards, or for gardens, or for vineyards; Yea, all things which come of the earth, in the season thereof, are made for the benefit and the use of man, both to please the eye and to gladden the heart; Yea, for food and for raiment, for taste and for smell, to strengthen the body and to enliven the soul.
>
> And it pleaseth God that he hath given all these things unto man; for unto this end were they made to be used, with judgment, not to excess, neither by extortion. (D&C 59:15–20)

Pleasure—"to please the eye and to gladden the heart"—is a purpose of creation, and the gratification of our human senses—"for taste and for smell"—delights the Creator. However, He stipulates that our pleasure in the creation must be guided by gratitude and good cheer, rather than the prideful and self-centered thinking that often animates loud laughter.

Some of the pleasures we instinctively identify as "safe" are those which we naturally associate with a turning to God or a subsuming of self in some larger whole. For instance, viewing the beauty of a sunset, a mountain range, or a field of wildflowers often inclines our hearts to God in thanksgiving because we recognize the divine origin of these natural wonders. I will never forget when my oldest son first learned to pray, at the tender age of eighteen months; without any prompting from me or his mother, Gabriel would wax poetic in gratitude "for flowers, and for butterflies, and for the beautiful earth." He could recognize that the intricate workings of nature had a cause beyond himself and felt his heart drawn, in thanks, to the Creator. Other pleasures draw us into a closer relation with God's sons and daughters. Singing in a choir, for example, or participating in a well-choreographed dance, or observing others performing as a group might lead us to feel intimately connected to other participants and to experience what Barbara Ehrenreich calls the "incommunicable thrill of the group deliberately united in joy and exaltation."[12] These pleasurable activities invite us to lose ourselves in a collective and to see ourselves as part of a larger human family, and so we naturally incorporate congregational hymns and other forms of corporate action into our worship services.

However, even our participation in a choir or our appreciation of nature might be perverted by pride; it is not the type of activity that sanctifies pleasure but our motive for participating in it. To wit, I have known some whose love of nature has led them to declare, with Emily Dickinson,

> Some keep the Sabbath going to Church –
> I keep it, staying at Home –
> With a Bobolink for a Chorister –
> And an Orchard, for a Dome –[13]

12. Barbara Ehrenreich, *Dancing in the Streets: A History of Collective Joy*, 16.

13. Emily Dickinson, "324: Some keep the Sabbath going to Church," 153.

The beauties of nature might lead us to give thanks, like my toddler son, for God's goodness. But they might also become a pretext for rejecting the expressed will of Christ, that we gather together on the Sabbath to partake the emblems of His death (D&C 59:9). Participating in a choir might lead us to feel a greater sense of unity with those with whom we are striving to harmonize, or it might—and to my shame, I can attest to this motive from personal experience—lead us to sing stridently and just a tad louder than necessary, so that an individual voice can be distinguished from the group. As President Ezra Taft Benson warned, "Our motives for the things we do are where the sin is manifest," whether that motive is a selfish desire to spend the Sabbath in recreation or a prideful impulse to make the choir a showcase for our own (imagined) virtuosic talents.[14] There is no safety in selecting our pleasures from a pre-selected menu, even when they might seem as innocuous as watching the sunset or singing in a choir.

Conversely, pleasures that might seem transgressive (sometimes for cultural rather than doctrinal reasons, like the waltz) can be the means of drawing our souls into communion with friends and family or with God—just as the plays of Shakespeare, despite their crude, lewd, and violent episodes, have provided moral instruction to leaders of the Church for decades. If I were to appraise one of my favorite novels, Stuart Turton's *The 7 ½ Deaths of Evelyn Hardcastle*, in the same way that motion pictures are evaluated, it would definitely be an R-rated production. Turton's thriller is a murder mystery that portrays episodes of drug abuse, torture, and attempted rape in frank language, and as I read it for the first time, I found myself wondering whether I

14. Ezra Taft Benson, "Beware of Pride."

could continue reading in good conscience—whether it
was appropriate to find pleasure in Turton's representation
of tragedy and evil. I might still be wondering if not for a
surprise turn in the novel's final few pages (which I won't
spoil for you, dear reader) that brought tears to my eyes and
left me pondering—for days—the power and significance
of the Atonement of Jesus Christ. Similarly, I once recoiled
in horror at the thought of reading the vivid representa-
tions of child abuse, sexual violence, and lynching that fill
historical and fictional accounts of the suffering endured by
Black Americans as a result of racism and slavery, but I now
rejoice to read such works because I find they provide understanding necessary "to lead out in abandoning attitudes
and actions of prejudice" and also because I take delight
in the beauty of their language and sentiments.[15] Content
I previously rejected as problematic or even abhorrent has
become a pleasurable and uplifting source of perspective
on vital moral questions, increasing my empathy for other
members of the human family.

Perhaps you can believe that exposure to such materials is necessary but object to the idea that such exposure
could or should be pleasurable. However, given our natural
aversion to that which is painful or simply not enjoyable,
it is doubtful that we will ever devote appropriate time and
energy to important endeavors in which we cannot find
pleasure. Elder Sterling W. Sill declared as much in general
conference, observing that

> Shakespeare said, "No profit comes where there is no plea-
> sure taken." You can't do very well that which you don't enjoy
> doing. If we don't get great pleasure out of our families, we
> should repent, because we are doing something wrong. If the
> work of the Lord seems burdensome and makes us weary, or

---

15. Russell M. Nelson, "Let God Prevail."

if we don't get exhilaration and uplift out of that part of the
work of the world that life has given us to do, then we should
repent. We need some more powerful satisfactions from life.[16]
I offer this invocation of Shakespeare somewhat facetiously
because—as I have already suggested—the appearance of
a quotation in a general conference address does not necessarily indicate that the source material from which the
quotation has been drawn is an unimpeachable fount of
moral truth; Shakespeare was considered a moral reprobate
before he became a regular contributor to the semi-annual
sermons of prophets and apostles. However, Shakespeare's
counsel in this instance is sound, despite the misogyny
and other questionable moral positions advanced by Elder
Sill's source material in *The Taming of the Shrew*. We must
seek for and find pleasure in the most important pursuits
of our lives or we will be liable to resent and neglect those
activities—to our detriment.

Unless we purposefully embrace pleasure, even eternally important activities might—as Elder Sill warned—become burdensome or make us weary. Few phrases convey
the truthfulness of that warning better than a statement
inaccurately attributed to Queen Victoria of England,
who supposedly said that to endure sexual intercourse with
her husband, she would "lie back and think of England."
Producing an heir to the throne is not, for most of the
world's inhabitants, a civic or sexual duty, but the broader
sentiment—that sex is an obligation to be endured rather
than a pleasure which unifies and strengthens a relation-

---

16. Sterling W. Sill, "Hold Up Your Hands." Although Elder
Sill uses quotation marks, he paraphrases this passage from *The
Taming of the Shrew*, which actually reads, "No profit grows
where is no pleasure ta'en." See William Shakespeare, *The Taming
of the Shrew*, *The Complete Works of Shakespeare*, 116.

ship—is felt in far too many marriages. When Belinda
Marden Pratt argued, in 1854, that women should not
have sex during pregnancy, she spoke in circuitous terms,
condemning "anything calculated to disturb, irritate,
weary, or exhaust" the pregnant body. The implication is
that intercourse with her husband, Elder Parley P. Pratt,
was sometimes a matter of duty rather than delight: "Or
in other words, indulgence should not be merely for
pleasure, or wanton desires, but mainly for the purpose
of procreation."[17] The sentiment misattributed to Queen
Victoria has been so widely remembered because it reflects
the real experience of women like Belinda Marden Pratt.

If sex is disturbing, irritating, wearisome, and exhausting
for one or both parties, then it is not a dangerously pleasurable indulgence or a celebration of marital unity but a
burdensome duty to be endured, whether for England, for
God, or for a spouse whose larger libido might reflexively
be condemned as a sign of carnality and sinfulness. But
that attitude toward intercourse is both a function of our
instinctual mistrust of pleasure and a guarantee that the
sexual relationship intended to be "a symbol of total union"
will instead be a source of contention and dissatisfaction in
marriage.[18] Unless we are reconciled to pleasure and ready
to welcome it into our lives as a divinely-given gift, we will
never enjoy a fulness of the joy our Heavenly Parents have
ordained for us in the eternal institution of marriage.

Pratt's Victorian perspective still lingers in Church discourse, which affirms the divinity of intercourse between husband and wife but places far more emphasis on chastity prior
to marriage than the appropriate exercise of sexual agency

---

17. Belinda Marden Pratt, *Defence of Polygamy, by a Lady of
Utah, in a Letter to Her Sister in New Hampshire*, 4.

18. Jeffrey R. Holland, "Of Souls, Symbols, and Sacraments."

afterwards. The idea that sex is "mainly for the purpose of procreation" finds currency in *The Family: A Proclamation to the World*, which endorses intercourse only insofar as it serves "to multiply and replenish the earth."[19] Before his call to the apostleship, Elder Holland instructed BYU students as to "why human intimacy is such a serious matter," and it is.[20] But if the most frequent messages from the Church are that sex should be avoided before marriage and that sex should be seriously and solemnly endured after marriage solely for the means of producing children, we run all manner of risks.

First, and most importantly, married men and women who take pleasure in sex might wonder if that pleasure is somehow illegitimate—a sign of sinfulness. To abandon pleasure to the Adversary, when the Lord has explicitly and repeatedly stated that pleasure is an intended outcome of creation—Eden was "pleasant to the sight, and good for food" (Gen. 2:9); our bodies are made "to please the eye" and "for taste and for smell" (D&C 59:18–19)—is blasphemous, a rejection of God's gifts. Those who accept that God created the human body should also accept that He meant us to take pleasure in the use of our bodies because while most reproductive organs in male and female bodies serve multiple purposes, scientists agree that the "only known function of the clitoris is sexual pleasure."[21] Pleasure, in other words, is a divinely intended outcome of intercourse, separate and apart from the conception of children.[22]

---

19. "The Family: A Proclamation to the World."

20. Holland, "Of Souls, Symbols, and Sacraments."

21. Anne Bolin and Patricia Whelehan, *Perspectives on Human Sexuality*, 109.

22. Riane Eisler notes that both pleasure and the propagation of the species were recognized as important outcomes of intercourse by past generations of religious thinkers: "For

Additionally, when ecclesiastical messaging about sex centers around the dual mandates of chastity before marriage and the conception of children after marriage, the development of sexual agency in Church members is likely to be stunted. Chastity messaging that frames sexuality as a danger to be feared, while linking marital sex to the conception of children or the morally suspect "needs" of a spouse with higher desire, makes intercourse a matter of duty. Neither approach is conducive to the healthy exercise of moral and sexual agency.

When we characterize sex as a duty or associate it with the "needs" of a spouse, we abdicate our agency and risk the condemnation of God. To members of the Church in Missouri the Lord declared:

> For behold, it is not meet that I should command in all things; for he that is compelled in all things, the same is a slothful and not a wise servant; wherefore he receiveth no reward. Verily I say, men should be anxiously engaged in a good cause, and do many things of their own free will, and bring to pass much righteousness; For the power is in them, wherein they are agents unto themselves. And inasmuch as men do good they shall in nowise lose their reward. (D&C 58:26–28)

If sex is always in response to God's commandment to multiply and replenish the earth or a spouse's expressed preference or their perceived "need," we are not divinely

---

our ancestors *both* life and pleasure were within the realm of the sacred." She contends that "there is no logical reason for disassociating sexuality—and sexual pleasure—from the process of life giving and regeneration," and I would add that there is also no theological reason for doing so, even though we sometimes speak and act as though there is. See Riane Eisler, *Sacred Pleasure: Sex, Myth, and the Politics of the Body*, 59.

empowered agents free "to act for [ourselves]" but objects "to be acted upon" (2 Ne. 2:26). Being anxiously engaged in the exercise of sexual agency might compound our extant anxieties, but our bodies must be given to our spouses as an expression of "free will" if we hope to "do good" and "bring to pass much righteousness." A mutually pleasurable sexual relationship between husband and wife is a "good cause" that warrants our investment of time, attention, and energy; indeed, the moment when man and woman are "both naked" but "not ashamed" and become "one flesh" was the original good cause of creation (Gen. 2:24–25). Unless we can see beyond the commandment to conceive and the compelling cultural imperative to service the sexual "needs" of a spouse, we will never be free to exercise moral agency in our sexual relationships.

A reluctance to embrace sexual agency and sexual pleasure after marriage is, at least in part, a function of inherited messaging on chastity before marriage. To paraphrase a popular saying, transitioning from "No, no, no!" to "Go, go, go!" overnight is unlikely to be a successful proposition for those whose pre-marital abstinence has been driven by fear-based messaging about the dangers of sexuality. Elder Holland called attention to the fear-inducing metaphors associated with sexuality in this excerpt of a 1998 general conference address, which begins with a quotation from the historians Will and Ariel Durant:

> "A youth boiling with hormones will wonder why he should not give full freedom to his sexual desires; [but] if he is unchecked by custom, morals, or laws, he may ruin his life before he . . . understand[s] that sex is a river of fire that must be banked and cooled by a hundred restraints if it is not to consume in chaos both the individual and the group."

A more important scriptural observation is offered by the writer of Proverbs: "Can a man take fire in his bosom, and his clothes not be burned? Can one go upon hot coals, and his feet not be burned? . . . Whoso committeth adultery . . . destroyeth his own soul. A wound and dishonour shall he get; and his reproach shall not be wiped away."

Why is this matter of sexual relationships so severe that fire is almost always the metaphor, with passion pictured vividly in flames? What is there in the potentially hurtful heat of this that leaves one's soul—or the whole world, for that matter—destroyed if that flame is left unchecked and those passions unrestrained? What is there in all of this that prompts Alma to warn his son Corianton that sexual transgression is "an abomination in the sight of the Lord; yea, most abominable above all sins save it be the shedding of innocent blood or denying the Holy Ghost?"[23]

If the choice to be chaste before marriage is motivated by fear and lurid images of world-destroying infernos or molten lava, newlyweds are hardly likely to be reassured that the river of fire has been transformed, during their fifteen minutes at the altar, into a swimming pool and that the

---

23. Jeffrey R. Holland, "Personal Purity." This framing of sexuality as a danger to be feared has often been repeated. Elder Holland was actually echoing counsel given four years earlier, to a smaller audience, by President Gordon B. Hinckley, who had quoted the same passage from Will and Ariel Durant. Other Church leaders have amplified this rhetoric of fiery danger. Speaking of sexual temptation, Bruce C. Hafen declared that "the American people have never been in greater moral bondage than in this time when they glory in being free to pursue pleasure in any form they fancy as if there will never be any tomorrow. . . . If the H-bomb symbolizes our age, we are playing now not just with fire, but with nuclear power." See Gordon B. Hinckley, "Codes and Covenants," and Bruce C. Hafen, "The Gospel and Romantic Love."

water is fine—Come on in![24] John testified that "there is no fear in love," but the converse is also true: there is no love in fear (1 John 4:18).[25] If, as a Church, we want to cultivate loving marriages in which sexual relationships are a source of strength and not anxiety, we need to more fully embrace scriptures and metaphors that frame sexual pleasure in positive terms, as the God-given gift it is.

The same scriptural sources that Elder Holland cites might also called upon for messages that frame sexual-

---

24. I have a holy envy for language used in the Church of England, when husband and wife present themselves before the altar to be married, and wish that the phrase "With my body I thee worship" found place in our teachings on marriage. Such language might do much to persuade newlyweds that the water is, indeed, fine.

25. Notably, members of the Church have been concerned for decades about the tendency to frame sexuality in fear-based language. In a 1983 reflection on male sexuality, Marvin Rytting wrote, "The Mormon model combines reverence and fear, with the focus on the fear. We are taught that sex is dangerous, and therefore that women are dangerous. We are taught to distrust ourselves and each other. We are told that sex is a powerful force that can sweep us away at any moment, destroying our lives." And seven years earlier, Kenneth Cannon provided a similar perspective, based on twenty years of service in Brigham Young University's College of Family Living: "The instructor of a BYU religion class had his students search the teachings of the 'living prophets' concerning the goals of sex education. They found only one goal—chastity—which may be achieved at a cost of strong fears and negative attitudes toward sex, with such fears and attitudes causing sexual maladjustment and dissatisfaction in marriage." See Marvin Rytting, "Sexual Scripts: Rewriting the Lines," 16; and Kenneth L. Cannon, "Needed: An LDS Philosophy of Sex," 58.

ity in positive terms. In addition to proverbs that warn against adultery in fiery language, there are verses seldom or never cited that promote the pursuit of sexual pleasure in marriage, including this encouragement: "Rejoice with the wife of thy youth. Let her be as the loving hind and pleasant roe; let her breasts satisfy thee at all times; and be thou ravished always with her love" (Prov. 5:18–19).[26] Indeed, the writer of Proverbs saw sexual gratification in marriage as a safeguard against sins such as adultery; if husband and wife are mutually satisfied with their sexual relationship, the writer asks in the following verse, "why wilt thou, my son, be ravished with a strange woman, and embrace the bosom of a stranger?" (v. 20). Proverbs does warn against the dangers of adultery, but it also urges husband and wife to seek and to find pleasure in erotic and sensual encounters with one another, promising that pleasure will promote fidelity in marriage.

Similarly, Alma's scriptural warning to his son Corianton against sexual sin might be weighed against his more sex-positive messaging to another son, Shiblon. In seminary

---

26. The Song of Solomon likewise offers an extended meditation on love that might not be revelation but has long been included in both Jewish and Christian canons as an allegorical expression of love between God and a covenant people. Some have suggested that the poems in this book "were in fact written as wedding poems, but the content of most of them leads one to conclude that the free enjoyment of the pleasures of love and not marriage is what the poets had in view." Rather than invent increasingly tortured rationales for its inclusion in the Bible, we would be wise to recognize that the Song of Solomon has persisted within the canon *because* it recognizes sexual pleasure as a divine gift. See Robert Alter, "Introduction to the Song of Solomon," 584.

and other settings, youth are encouraged to "bridle all your passions," but in my experience, we speak of that admonition to Shiblon only in the negative language of restraint, without really examining the metaphor's broader positive implications (Alma 38:12).[27] A bridle is used to direct a horse's head so that someone walking alongside the horse or riding on its back can control its movements and guide it toward the desired destination. To bridle passions, then, is to proactively and intentionally direct their movements toward a desired destination. But the broader ecclesiastical discourse has effectively suggested that our passions are so dangerous that, like a rogue horse, they must be locked up in a barn until marriage, when a spouse will bridle them for us and direct our sexual impulses to their proper destination. Alma's counsel to an apparently unmarried son is more liberal, inviting Shiblon to take control of his own passions in the present rather than stifling them until an unknown future arrives.

The intended outcome of the counsel offered by Alma and Elder Holland is the same: chastity before marriage and fidelity afterwards. But we have collectively gravitated toward negative metaphors for sexuality to our collective detriment. The river of fire that youth fearfully avoided before marriage will still be a source of anxiety and apparent danger after marriage, prompting husband and wife to consider their own desires and the desires of their spouse with suspicion. Framing sexuality as a river of fire suggests that sexuality is more powerful than our agency, but we are, necessarily, stronger than the desires that inform

---

27. Similarly, the takeaway from chastity lessons involving cake or brownies is more often a fear of sexual degradation or contamination than a sense of gratitude for or excitement about human sexuality.

us—we are the whole of which sexuality is merely a part. Passions that we control, as a subordinated part of our whole soul, and that have been carefully and intentionally led toward the destination of a mutually fulfilling marital union, might be given freer rein within the context of a marriage relationship, allowing expressions of sexuality previously held in check at a walking or trotting pace— gazing, conversing, imagining, holding hands, hugging, kissing—to be given their head, at a canter and then a gallop. Galloping on horseback might induce a bit of anxiety and places a rider at some small risk of accident and even death, but it is a risk willingly undertaken in order to progress toward a goal and for the sheer pleasure of riding, whereas falling into a river of fire is always and only a disaster. If chastity before marriage and fidelity after marriage are achieved at the cost of making the divine gift of sexual pleasure into a source of fearful anxiety, we concede to Satan an unearned victory and forfeit the fulness of joy that comes when body and spirit strive together toward a single goal as a unified, integrated soul.

Although members and local leaders of The Church of Jesus Christ of Latter-day Saints commonly emphasize the warnings of Church leaders, there is a complementary body of teachings celebrating sexual pleasure as a source of joy in marriage that might be amplified alongside those warnings. The *General Handbook* outlining Church policies declares that "physical intimacy between husband and wife is intended to be beautiful and sacred. It is ordained of God for the creation of children and for the expression of love between husband and wife."[28] Readers of the *Handbook* might not associate pleasure with the "sacred,"

28. *General Handbook: Serving in The Church of Jesus Christ of Latter-day Saints*, 38.6.4, 38.6.5.

but surely it is implicit in that which is "beautiful" and an "expression of love." When Elder Boyd K. Packer spoke of the "procreative power," he noted that "the process through which life is conceived should be accompanied by feelings of such depth and attraction that they draw the individual to seek a repetition of them."[29] Again, the word *pleasure* is unspoken but clearly implicit in this teaching that endorses feelings we instinctively seek to repeat.

Instead of *pleasure*, prophets most frequently use the word *joy*, as when President Russell M. Nelson explained, "God implanted strong appetites within us for nourishment and love, vital for the human family to be perpetuated. When we master our appetites within the bounds of Gods' laws, we can enjoy longer life, greater love, and consummate joy."[30] To consummate a marriage is to engage in sexual intercourse, and the consummate joy spoken of here is an embrace of appetite in keeping with Alma's counsel to bridle our passions. These prophetic teachings provide a doctrinal framework for celebrating and reclaiming sexual pleasure that could be taught more regularly in our local meetings, alongside the ever-present warnings against misusing our sexual capacities. John Gottman has suggested that marital relationships need five instances of positive feedback for every negative instance in order to thrive, and I would argue that the same must be true of how we share positive and negative prophetic messaging on sexuality if we hope to thrive in this area as a community and as individuals.[31]

---

29. Boyd K. Packer, *The Things of the Soul*, 106.

30. Russell M. Nelson, "Decisions for Eternity."

31. John Gottman writes,

As part of our research we carefully charted the amount of time couples spent fighting versus interacting positively—

Prophetic messaging on sexuality—like prophetic messaging on the Sabbath—has shifted in recent years from a rules-based approach to an agency-focused emphasis on the application of gospel principles in widely varying circumstances. In the same way that President Nelson encouraged Church members to shift from lists of Sabbath-acceptable and Sabbath-prohibited activities to a more mature consideration of what sign any given activity sends to God about our regard for His holy day, revisions to *For the Strength of Youth* manuals reflect a shift from detailed protocols to a guide for making inspired choices related to sexuality and other matters. When *For the Strength of Youth* was first released in 1965, it contained a comprehensive dress code including counsel such as "Pants for young women are not desirable attire for shopping, at school, in the library, in cafeterias or restaurants," and "It is not appropri-

---

touching, smiling, paying compliments, laughing, etc. Across the board we found there was a very specific ratio that exists between the amount of positivity and negativity in a stable marriage, whether it is marked by validation, volatility, or conflict avoidance.

That magic ratio is *5 to 1*. In other words, as long as there is five times as much positive feeling and interaction between husband and wife as there is negative, we found the marriage was likely to be stable. It was based on this ratio that we were able to predict whether couples were likely to divorce: in very unhappy couples, there tended to be more negative than positive interaction.

While I cannot provide the quantitative data that Gottman offers, I suspect that the ratio of positive to negative messaging, with respect to sexuality in Church teachings at all levels, is underwater. See John Gottman and Nan Silver, *Why Marriages Succeed or Fail: And How You Can Make Yours Last*, 57.

ate for young men to wear extremely tight-fitting pants."[32] The 2001 edition of that pamphlet cautioned, "Immodest clothing includes short shorts and skirts, tight clothing, shirts that do not cover the stomach, and other revealing attire. Young women should wear clothing that covers the shoulder and avoid clothing that is low-cut in the front or the back or revealing in any other manner. Young men should also maintain modesty in their appearance."[33] But instead of a proscriptive list of wardrobe dos and don'ts, the 2022 pamphlet invites each reader to "ask yourself, 'Am I honoring my body as a sacred gift from God?'"[34] This shift, from a detailed dress code that regards the body as a dangerous sexual provocation which must be covered to an invitation to exercise sexual agency in consultation with deity, reflects a movement away from constraint and a fear-inducing fire metaphor toward agency and a more sex-positive bridling metaphor.

Rather than fixating on specific clothing items or sexual activities and the question of whether they are prohibited or acceptable before and after marriage, prophets are now inviting Church members to ask whether their choices reflect a reverence for God, for their own bodies, and for those with whom they are interacting. Reverence is not incompatible with pleasure and need not be solemn or serious; consider the humorous anecdotes with which Elder Holland and other apostles or prophets often begin their

---

32. *For the Strength of Youth . . . : LDS Standards*, 6–7. The First Presidency letter that prefaced this pamphlet, signed by Presidents David O. McKay, Hugh B. Brown, and N. Eldon Tanner, declared that "all rules and regulations, in fact all laws, especially the laws of God, are made for the benefit of the people."

33. *For the Strength of Youth: Fulfilling Our Duty to God*, 15–16.

34. *For the Strength of Youth: A Guide for Making Choices*, 24.

invitations to worship, which lead us to reverence by means of humor, playfulness, and delight.[35] Indeed, Jewish rabbis have long regarded sexual intercourse between husband and wife as an expression of reverence for God and taught that "the night of the Sabbath is to be devoted to conjugal

---

35. One of my favorite moments in more than forty years of general conference addresses came in April 2022, when Elder Holland read a letter

> from my eight-year-old friend Marin Arnold, written when she was seven. I will translate for you her early reformed Egyptian:
>
>> Dear Bishop
>> generle confrins
>> was Boring why
>> Do we half to
>> Do it? tell me why
>> Sinserlie, Marin
>> Arnold.
>
> Well, Marin, the talk I am about to give will undoubtedly bore you again. But when you write your bishop to complain, it is important to that you tell him my name is "Kearon. Elder Patrick Kearon."

This light-hearted introduction to a talk on coping with adversity featured role-playing, self-deprecation, and teasing, but it was also prepared and delivered in a spirit of reverence. To say that sexual interactions should reflect a reverence for God, for the bodies He has created for us, and for one another is not to insist on solemnity. Reverence in such a setting can—and perhaps should—be similarly playful, reflecting our familiarity with the Lord's character. God's own sense of humor is abundantly evident in the scriptures: Remember, for instance, the angel's first words to Gideon, who was hiding "from the Midianites" when the divine messenger declared, "The Lord is with thee, thou mighty man of valour" (Judg. 6:11–12). See Jeffrey R. Holland, "Fear Not: Believe Only!"

pleasures."[36] Jewish legend also holds that Adam had a wife before Eve's creation, named Lilith, who was exiled from Eden because "she took offense at the recumbent posture he demanded" she assume during intercourse, asking, "Why must I lie beneath you?"[37] However, our own approach to sex and sexual pleasure should be governed neither by prohibitions ("This sexual position is incompatible with goodness and Eden!") nor positive mandates ("Have sex every Sunday evening!") but by a desire to enter more fully into a loving relationship with God, our spouse, and the bodies created for us, which will lead each of us to a range of decisions about sex and sexual pleasure because our bodies, our spouses, and our relationships with God are so varied.[38]

---

36. Louis Ginzberg, *The Legends of the Jews*, 444.

37. As quoted in Lilly Rivlin, "Lilith," 7.

38. As Elder James E. Talmage taught in 1913, and as Elder Holland reiterated during his time as president of BYU, a love of and appreciation for our bodies is fundamental Restoration doctrine, without which we would be adrift in the larger sea of Christian teachings:

> We have been taught . . . to look upon these bodies of ours as gifts from God. We Latter-day Saints do not regard the body as something to be condemned, something to be abhorred. . . . We regard [the body] as the sign of our royal birthright. . . . We recognize . . . that those who kept not their first estate . . . were denied that inestimable blessing. . . . We believe that these bodies . . . may be made, in very truth, the temple of the Holy Ghost. . . .
>
> It is peculiar to the theology of the Latter-day Saints that we regard the body as an essential part of the soul. Read your dictionaries, the lexicons, and encyclopedias, and you will find that nowhere [in Christianity], outside of the Church of Jesus Christ, is the solemn and eternal truth taught that the soul of man is the body and the spirit combined.

As quoted in Holland, "Of Souls, Symbols, and Sacraments."

Only as we shift away from the false binary of safe and risky pleasures, with its inevitable and legalistic list of dos and don'ts, will we be able to act as agents in bridling our own passions. Rather than outsourcing our agency and relying on cultural signposting that identifies Shakespeare and the waltz and choral singing and sex as either uplifting or degrading pleasures, we will ask whether and how our participation in these pleasurable activities communicates our reverence and respect for one another, for God, and for His creation. Instead of fearfully shunning or shaming activities that powerfully stimulate our senses, we will seek revelation as to whether these experiences will help us progress toward the fulness of joy intended for us by Heavenly Parents. Cultivating the spiritual maturity that living prophets have encouraged us to develop, through revisions to *For the Strength of Youth* and new guidance about the Sabbath, will draw us into closer and more loving relationships with God, with creation, and with others.

4. Revelation and Restraint

Seeking revelation about the place of pleasure in our lives and acting on answers received will lead to a wide range of decisions and outcomes because of the different circumstances in which we live and make choices. As a youth, I made the decision that I only wanted to kiss the young woman I would marry—not because I feared that kissing many young women would lead me into an impassioned frenzy or stimulate desires that I could not control, but because I wanted that pleasurable expression of love to be a sign of my esteem for her and for our relationship and for the divine imperative to bridle our passions. As it happens, I shared my first kiss with a young woman named Alana Ogarek, and twenty-three years later, she is still the only woman whose lips have touched mine. But that first kiss came a scant three weeks after we began conversing, and if Alana or I had made different decisions, I might easily have kissed half a dozen young women on my way to the altar. In other words, the outcome (only kissing one person) was less important than the process (seeking divine guidance about when and why and with whom it was appropriate for me to enjoy the pleasure of a kiss). As we try to be intentional about our relationship to pleasure and to exercise our agency in ways that communicate a reverence for God, we will come to a wide range of inspired conclusions about what is appropriate in our varying circumstances. An increased capacity for personal revelation must also be accompanied by increased humility, so that we resist the temptation to impose our own paradigm for pleasure on others.

There can be no single, standard answer for how and when and why we welcome pleasure into our lives, but if we are truly seeking to be guided by revelation we should, on occasion, be surprised by the Spirit's counsel.[1] In the absence of surprise—a sense that we have been invited to do something other than what we would otherwise, of ourselves, undertake—we can never be certain that we have not simply acted according to our own preferences.[2] Most often, the Spirit invites us to forsake our own com-

---

1. Joseph Smith encouraged the Saints to recognize the divine origin of these surprising admonitions and insights: "A person may profit by noticing the first intimation of the Spirit of Revelation for instance when you feel pure Inteligence flowing unto you it may give you sudden strokes of ideas that by noticeing it you may find it fulfilled the same day or soon. (I,E,) those things that were presented unto your minds by the Spirit of God will come to pass and thus by learning the Spirit of God. & understanding it you may grow into the principle of Revelation. until you become perfect in Christ Jesus." See Joseph Smith, "Discourse, between circa 26 June and circa 2 July 1839, as Reported by Willard Richards," 21–22.

2. Søren Kierkegaard writes, "Although a revelation is a paradoxical factor which surpasses man's understanding, one can nevertheless understand this much, which has, moreover, proved to be the case everywhere: that a man is called by a revelation to go out in the world, to proclaim the Word, to act and to suffer, to a life of uninterrupted activity as the Lord's messenger. But that a man should be called by a revelation to sit back and enjoy his possessions undisturbed, in active literary *far niente*, momentarily clever, and afterwards as publisher and editor of the uncertainties of his own cleverness: that is something approaching blasphemy." The larger point here is that we recognize revelation (and a sense of authority outside ourselves) only when we receive a message in opposition to our "own cleverness." As a rule, such messages ask us to sacrifice corporeal pleasure for "a life of uninterrupted activity as the Lord's messenger," but I would suggest that if and when our own cleverness becomes preoccupied with sacrifice, we should, on occasion, be surprised by a divine invitation to "sit

fort and pleasure to serve and uplift others. C. S. Lewis conjectured that

> if our expenditure on comforts, luxuries, amusements, etc., is up to the standard common among those with the same income as our own, we are probably giving away too little. If our charities do not at all pinch or hamper us, I should say they are too small. There ought to be things we should like to do and cannot do because our charitable expenditure excludes them.[3]

Just as Jesus invited "a certain ruler" to "sell all that thou hast," so He will invite each of us, individually, to cast our two mites into the treasury and give up the pleasures that keep us from a more consecrated life in His service (Luke 18:18–23). We should, occasionally, be surprised by the Spirit's call to give up food and drink and fast on a Tuesday; to put away the mindless gratification of social media feeds; to donate money and time; or to wake up earlier than we might wish. These unsought promptings to give up a favorite pastime or pleasure in the Lord's service are an excellent sign that we are living according to the spirit of revelation.

We often hear in Church meetings of such promptings to defer or reject some minor pleasure so that the speaker or teacher could be better prepared to offer service.[4] But we should also be sensitive to promptings that unexpectedly

---

back and enjoy"—that the answer to Sarah's question is yes. See Søren Kierkegaard, *The Living Thoughts of Kierkegaard*, 93.

3. C. S. Lewis, *Mere Christianity*, 86.

4. For example, President Michelle D. Craig, of the Young Women General Presidency, recalled an impression to "stop looking at your phone when you are waiting in lines," and explained that following this counsel allowed her "to truly see and connect with another person who needed it." Stories of this sort are commonplace in weekly sacrament and Sunday school

encourage us to embrace pleasure. As a young missionary newly arrived in the Brasil João Pessoa mission, I took great pride in the hard work of contacting strangers and teaching them about the gospel of Jesus Christ; I badly wanted to follow every mission rule and to be diligent in the work of salvation. Walking down the street one day, on our way to the home of a member with whom we hoped to visit, my senior companion suggested that we.stop to play with a pack of children jumping rope in the cobblestone street who were clearly too young to make baptismal covenants. I scoffed at Elder Baker's suggestion: how could we justify spending fifteen or thirty minutes playing jump rope when we were supposed to be on the Lord's errand? But he insisted, and so I dropped my backpack and asked the children if we could swing the jump rope for them. Their enthusiasm was infectious, and I quickly found myself having fun, smiling and chanting along with them as they took turns jumping. Ten or fifteen minutes after we'd stopped to play with the children, a young woman named Isiegly emerged from one of the homes along the street and thanked us for our kindness to the children, who attended daycare in her home. She asked who we were, and when we explained our mission as representatives of the restored Church of Jesus Christ, Isiegly invited us to return after her daycare closed and share our message. She and her brother were baptized several weeks later, and when I left Brazil, she was serving as the ward's Relief Society President—all because my wise senior companion was quick to observe a prompting to put aside our labors and enjoy a period of play.

Because of its conclusion—a teaching opportunity and a baptism—this story might suggest that play and pleasure

---

meetings, as well as in the general conferences of the Church. See Michelle D. Craig, "Eyes to See."

are only valuable as means to an obviously sanctified end. But Elder Baker's inspired suggestion that we stop to jump rope with young children still would have been divinely prompted even if Isiegly never introduced herself or expressed interest in learning more about the restored gospel of Jesus Christ. Decisions made by others must not be the standard by which we evaluate our own choices, and enjoying a bit of recreation with those children was a worthwhile activity whether or not it produced results measurable in the mission statistics. Latter-day Saints clearly accept the premise that work is worthwhile for its own sake. But, so, too, are pleasure and play: no quantifiable outcome is necessary to sanctify an afternoon in the park or a piece of pie.

Our cultural and ecclesiastical reverence for work occasionally borders on idolatry. Too often, we forget Jacob's admonition, "do not spend . . . your labor for that which cannot satisfy," and make work or busyness an end in and of itself (2 Ne. 9:51). But if an unwavering focus on pleasure is sinful, so is an eye single to the grindstone. As Daniel Markovits observes, American elites now regard work as the ultimate good, rejecting pleasure and recreation as a sign of virtue: "High society . . . valorizes industry and despises leisure" because intense work provides a moral justification for the unequal distribution of wealth in our American "meritocracy."[5] However, neither the Lord nor our hardworking pioneer forebears ever intended that industry should preclude recreation, rest, or pleasure.

Joseph Smith worked long and hard, but he also loved to wrestle with children and to laugh and to compete with other men in the stick pull. Brigham Young encouraged in-

---

5. Daniel Markovits, *The Meritocracy Trap: How America's Foundational Myth Feeds Inequality, Dismantles the Middle Class, and Devours the Elite*, 4, 96.

dustry, but he also urged the Saints to dance and to sing and to take pleasure in one another's company at the end of their labors by

> enjoying our pastimes. . . . That our minds may rest, and our bodies receive that recreation which is proper and necessary to keep up an equilibrium, to promote healthy action to the whole system. Let our minds sing for joy, and let life diffuse itself into every avenue of the body; for the object of our meeting is for its exercise, for its good.[6]

In this fallen world, we must labor in order to provide sustenance for ourselves and others. But in our embrace of work—a noble and necessary virtue—we sometimes forget that the Lord intends us to take pleasure in our bodies and to enjoy the abundance of His creation.

Pleasure can be a worthwhile end in and of itself, and not only when it is an unexpected pathway to achieving the love and unity that the Lord desires for us. My predisposition toward work and study and seriousness did not disappear when I returned home from my missionary service, and after I became a father, my children sometimes complained that Sabbath observance in our home felt more like restraint than rest; the worship I expected of them was immoderate, given their youth. I cheerfully disregarded their complaints for years and obtusely insisted that these very young children could learn to find joy in scripture study, service, and family history for the full twenty-four-hour period of the Sabbath. Imagine my surprise, then, when I felt impressed by the Spirit some years ago that I needed to begin the tradition of holding "family movie time" on the Sabbath day. As my children would attest, this prompting represented an abrupt about-face toward Sunday screen

---

6. Brigham Young, "Recreation, and the Proper Use of It," in *Journal of Discourses*, 1:29.

time on my part. But as we have made it a practice to gather and watch scenes from *Chariots of Fire* or *12 Angry Men* or *Encanto* or other uplifting films each week, I have observed that my children now regard the Sabbath as a delight and are more willing to engage in the worshipful work, which I had previously been trying to push them toward, once family movie time has ended each week.[7] Helping my children to find joy in the Sabbath through the pleasure of shared screen time was the unexpected and revelatory answer to a question I wasn't even asking, and while I can't point to a specific event, such as the baptism of Isiegly, as evidence that this turn toward pleasure was divinely inspired, the increased spirit of love and unity that fills our home each week on the Sabbath is evidence enough for me.

In suggesting that the Lord will, occasionally, surprise us with an invitation to make room in our lives for pleasure, it seems important to note that the pleasures which God most frequently endorses are those which bring us into community and fellowship with others. As the Psalmist declares, "Behold, how good and how pleasant"—how pleasurable, how Edenic—"it is for brethren to dwell together in unity!" (Ps. 133:1). The Lord may well invite us

---

7. Appropriately, one of the main characters in *Chariots of Fire*, Eric Liddell, insists that God approves of sport and recreation as well as service and worship. In a scene where he informs his sister, Jenny, that he will serve a proselyting mission to China only after he has completed his athletic career, Liddell explains, "I believe that God made me for a purpose: for China. But he also made me fast! And when I run, I feel His pleasure. To give it up would be to hold Him in contempt. You were right—it's not just fun. To win is to honor Him." Liddell insists that God takes pleasure in that which brings us pleasure and joy. See *Chariots of Fire*, directed by Hugh Hudson, 59:03–59:31.

to stop working and play with children or to gather together for uplifting entertainment or a delicious meal, but
we should be skeptical of any suggestion that He is calling
us to isolated, individual pleasures. Jesus may have snuck
off to pray and to commune with the Father in isolation,
but we don't have any record of Him hiding in a closet so
that He could turn water into wine for Himself or anoint
His own feet with spikenard. In seeking revelation, Elder
Dale G. Renlund has warned, "We do not 'ask amiss,' with
improper motives to promote our own agenda or to fulfill
our own pleasure."[8] The pleasures Jesus invites us to embrace are not self-serving but communal, not "our own"
but shared.

Because pleasure is intended to draw us together into
community and to facilitate the accomplishment of our
Savior's prayer, "that they may be one, even as we are one"
(John 17:22) or as Adam and Eve became "one" (Gen.
2:24), sensual enjoyments should never become causes
of contention or division. Better, in such a situation, to
metaphorically pluck out an eye or cut off a hand and forgo
the promised pleasure than to indulge and offend (Matt.
5:29–30). Even if we believe—even if we know!—that the
anticipated pleasure is innocuous and harmless before God,
Paul warns that we should defer or abstain out of charity
when others, whose faith might be shaken if they saw us
partake or participate, are present. Referring to the dietary
disagreements that produced so many arguments among
early Christians, Paul declared,

> It is good neither to eat flesh nor to drink wine, nor any
> thing whereby thy brother stumbleth, or is offended, or is
> made weak. Hast thou faith? Have it to thyself before God.
> Happy is he that condemneth not himself in that thing

---

8. Dale G. Renlund, "A Framework for Personal Revelation."

which he alloweth. And he that doubteth is damned if he
eat, because he eateth not of faith: for whatsoever is not of
faith is sin. (Rom. 14:21–23)

Paul speaks of debates prevalent among his contempo-
raries, over whether a vegetarian or an omnivorous diet is
acceptable to God, but he offers no hard guidelines (Rom.
14:2). In our day, similar arguments as to whether caffein-
ated soft drinks like Coke and Dr Pepper are prohibited
by the Word of Wisdom are common among Latter-day
Saints, and Paul's counsel seems to suggest that any who
believe such pleasures to be harmless can partake without
sinning. On the other hand, anyone who believes that
drinking those beverages is wrong will sin in doing so, *even
if they are in fact harmless.* The act is less important than the
sign we send to God in drinking or not drinking. Harmless
or not, Paul's point is simply that the pleasure of drinking
Dr Pepper is not worth offending another member of the
body of Christ; we should publicly eschew any pleasure
that might undermine the faith of others.

As a corollary principle, we should exercise restraint
and refrain from judging those whose pleasures offend our
sensibilities but not the Spirit. If we are among those who
believe that Coke and Dr Pepper are incompatible with
the Word of Wisdom, we should not condemn the Elders
Quorum President or Relief Society President who im-
bibes. I struggle to understand how people find pleasure
in films or novels identified as works of horror, but there
is nothing morally reprehensible about the short stories of
Edgar Allan Poe or films such as M. Night Shyamalan's *The
Village* and John Krasinski's *A Quiet Place*; my own failure
to find pleasure or inspiration in the genre does not give
me license to assess the righteousness of those who do. As
Paul counseled, "Let us not therefore judge one another

any more. . . . For he that in these things serveth Christ is acceptable to God, and approved of men" (Rom. 14:13, 18). Pleasure is divinely ordained and a gift from God, but it is not the only or the most important blessing bestowed by our Heavenly Father, and whenever pleasure distracts or distances us from eternal perspectives and priorities—including the unity that should prevail between members of the body of Christ—it must be deferred or sacrificed. Even as we seek for revelation to know when and how we might appropriately seek pleasure, we must exercise restraint and avoid condemning others whose inspired approach to sensual enjoyments differs from our own.

Conclusion

Living prophets have warned that pleasure can be a distraction from the scriptural imperatives "to prepare for eternity" and "improve our time while in this life" (Alma 34:33). Pointing to Esau's appetite as a cautionary tale, Elder David A. Bednar expressed concern that

> in the busyness of our daily lives and in the commotion of the contemporary world in which we live, we may be distracted from the eternal things that matter the most by making pleasure, prosperity, popularity, and prominence our primary priorities. Our short-term preoccupation with "the things of this world" and "the honors of men" may lead us to forfeit our spiritual birthright for far less than a mess of pottage.[1]

Similarly, President Russell M. Nelson declared that

> while the world insists that power, possessions, popularity, and pleasures of the flesh bring happiness, they do not! They cannot! What they do produce is nothing but a hollow substitute for "the blessed and happy state of those [who] keep the commandments of God."[2]

---

1. David A. Bednar, "Put on Thy Strength, O Zion."
2. Russell M. Nelson, "Overcome the World and Find Rest." Economists drawing conclusions about the eternally important work of parenting provide support for these claims, indicating that parental labor results in little direct pleasure but an overall happier life. Daniel Kahneman and his colleagues found that out of nineteen common daily experiences, parenting ranked sixteenth in terms of the pleasure it provided. However, Chris Herbst and John Ifcher observe that parents are generally happier than non-parents; pleasure-seeking is not a reliable path to durable happiness. See Daniel Kahneman, Alan B. Krueger, David A. Schkade, Norbert Schwarz, and Arthur

Prophets have clearly taught that pleasure-seeking can divert us from the covenant path. Our senses must never entice us to abandon the pressing business of eternity, so desires, appetites, and passions must be expressed or indulged only within covenantal bounds. The fulness of joy to be found in and through our covenants, which is our heavenly inheritance, must be augmented by, but cannot be reduced to, sensory input.

In the memorable parlance of President Dallin H. Oaks, pleasure can be a distraction from "better" and "best" activities with which we might fill our time.[3] We would do well, then, to heed the counsel given by the angel Michael to Adam in John Milton's *Paradise Lost*: "Judge not what is best / By pleasure."[4] And yet, if we reflexively shun pleasure as evil or as a source of temptation whereby our free will must inevitably be overmatched, we risk condemning that which God told us, in the beginning, is "very good": His Creation and our capacity to appreciate it through bodily senses (Gen. 1:31). Pleasure is part of the purpose for which we have been given eyes to see, ears to hear, and other sensory organs that enable us to appreciate the goodness of God's creation and our own embodiment.

Eyes and ears and tongues and fingers serve utilitarian ends, but if we reject their capacity for giving and receiving pleasure, we risk rejecting essential elements of our mortal experience. I love the story told by Edward Gibbon, of an ancient Roman: "A bag of shining leather, filled with pearls,

---

A. Stone, "A Survey Method for Characterizing Daily Life Experience: The Day Reconstruction Method," 1776–80; and Chris M. Herbst and John Ichfer, "The Increasing Happiness of US Parents," 529–51.

3. Dallin H. Oaks, "Good, Better, Best."

4. John Milton, *Paradise Lost*, XI, 603–4.

fell into the hands of a private soldier; he carefully preserved the bag, but he threw away its contents, judging that whatever was of no use could not possibly be of any value."[5] Because the leather bag could serve a practical purpose, the soldier prized it highly; because the pearls were strictly ornamental, he discarded them. This Roman soldier might be considered a foil to the woman who anointed Jesus's feet. Whereas she broke a container to extract every last drop of an ointment with little practical value, he prized a container's utility to such an extent that he could not recognize any beauty in its contents. The pleasure of beholding a pearl is impossible to quantify, and a pearl's value is subjective—a matter of beauty and desire, rather than measurable outcomes. But when the Savior instructed his disciples about the kingdom of heaven, He spoke of a merchant who "sold all that he had" to buy "one pearl of great price" (Matt. 13:46). Our capacity to recognize and appreciate beauty may, in part, determine our desire and ability to fully enter into the kingdom of heaven, whose glory is so effusively described in the final chapters of Revelation. Our bodies, like the world through which they move, in preparation for that glorious world to come, are endowed with both form and function. We should value both.

Pleasure must never be our priority, "the very first or prior thing" that comes before all others, but it should be valued as a divinely appointed blessing intended to draw us into more intimate and meaningful relation with God and with one another.[6] To reject pleasure entirely would be to forsake the doctrine of the Restoration, which embraces

---

5. Edward Gibbon, *The Decline and Fall of the Roman Empire*, 409.

6. Greg McKeown, *Essentialism: The Disciplined Pursuit of Less*, 16.

the Fall and materiality and our physical bodies as heavenly gifts. To reject pleasure entirely would be to side with those who characterized Jesus Christ as "a gluttonous man, and a winebibber," forgetting that He welcomed the woman anointing Him and taught that the pleasures of a feast, a fine robe, or a ring are appropriate expressions of welcome and celebration (Luke 7:34). To reject pleasure entirely would be to abandon sex and sexuality to the Adversary, being governed by fear rather than love in our strivings for marital intimacy. Pleasure can be good, better, and, when motivated by a love for God and others, even best. We must find a way to integrate it into our conception of the life that we are to have "more abundantly" through Jesus Christ and His gospel, lest we lapse into compulsive, immoderate patterns of abstinence and indulgence (John 10:10).

Joy is the end for which we were created, and pleasure is one facet of the fulness of joy that our Heavenly Parents intended us to receive. The Psalmist rejoiced,

> How excellent is thy lovingkindness, O God! therefore the children of men put their trust under the shadow of thy wings. They shall be abundantly satisfied with the fatness of thy house; and thou shalt make them drink of the river of thy pleasures. For with thee is the fountain of life: in thy light we shall see light. (Ps. 36:7–9)

This reassurance that our God delights in abundance and fatness is ultimately the same as that prophetically promised by Isaiah, who foretold that "the Lord shall comfort Zion: he will comfort all her waste places; and he will make her wilderness like Eden" (Isa. 51:3). To speak of Eden and of pleasure is redundant: *Eden* and *pleasure* are, in the original Hebrew, twin concepts. The Lord has pledged to restore Eden in the future, and as a reminder of that promise, He provides pleasures in the present, alleviating our path through the lone and dreary world in which we currently sojourn. His promises are sure, and His joy is comprehensive, encompassing both spiritual peace and sensory delight.

When Sarah asked, "Shall I have pleasure?" she sought reassurance that the Lord cared about her present, bodily happiness as well as her eternal, spiritual salvation. He did, and He does. Although the Savior calls his faithful to endure "the crosses of the world" and to be comforted with nails, we, too, can find solace and a temporary reprieve in the smell of spikenard or in the touch of a loved one or in other sensory enjoyments (2 Ne. 9:18). And if we are willing to receive the gifts He has prepared for the whole human family, we will find—with Sarah—that pleasure is among them.

Bibliography

Alter, Robert. "Introduction to the Song of Solomon." In *The Hebrew Bible: A Translation with Commentary*, translated and edited by Robert Alter. W. W. Norton, 2019.

Anderson, Elizabeth S. "John Stuart Mill and Experiments in Living." *Ethics* 102, no. 1 (October 1991): 4–26.

Ballard, M. Russell. "O that Cunning Plan of the Evil One." *Ensign*. November 2010.

Bednar, David A. "Put on Thy Strength, O Zion." *Liahona*. November 2022.

Benson, Ezra Taft. "Beware of Pride." *Ensign*. May 1989.

Bloom, Paul. *How Pleasure Works: The New Science of Why We Like What We Like*. W. W. Norton, 2010.

Bolin, Anne, and Patricia Whelehan. *Perspectives on Human Sexuality*. State University of New York Press, 1999.

Bryson, Bill. *Shakespeare: The World as Stage*. Harper Perennial, 2008.

Cannon, Kenneth L. "Needed: An LDS Philosophy of Sex." *Dialogue: A Journal of Mormon Thought* 10, no. 2 (1976): 57–61.

Carver, Charles S. "Pleasure as a Sign You Can Attend to Something Else: Placing Positive Feelings within a General Model of Affect." *Cognition and Emotion* 17 no. 2 (2003): 241–61.

Chariots of Fire. Directed by Hugh Hudson. 20th Century Fox, 1981.

Craig, Michelle D. "Eyes to See." *Liahona*. November 2020.

Croasmun, Matthew, and Miroslav Volf. *The Hunger for Home: Food & Meals in the Gospel of Luke*. Baylor University Press, 2022.

Davis, Andrew R. "Eden Revisited: A Literary and Theological Reading of Genesis 18:12–13." *The Catholic Biblical Quarterly* 78, no.4 (2016): 611–31.

Dickinson, Emily. "324: Some keep the Sabbath going to Church." In *The Complete Poems of Emily Dickinson*, edited by Thomas H. Johnson. Little, Brown and Company, 1960.

Dubé, Laurette, and Jordan L. Le Bel. "The Content and Structure of Laypeople's Concept of Pleasure." *Cognition and Emotion* 17, no. 2 (2003): 263–95.

Ehrenreich, Barbara. *Dancing in the Streets: A History of Collective Joy*. Metropolitan Books, 2007.

Eisler, Riane. *Sacred Pleasure: Sex, Myth, and the Politics of the Body*. HarperOne, 1996.

The First Presidency and Quorum of the Twelve Apostles of The Church of Jesus Christ of Latter-day Saints. "The Family: A Proclamation to the World." *Ensign*. November 1995.

For the Strength of Youth . . . : LDS Standards. The Church of Jesus Christ of Latter-day Saints, 1965.

For the Strength of Youth: A Guide for Making Choices. The Church of Jesus Christ of Latter-day Saints, 2022.

For the Strength of Youth: Fulfilling Our Duty to God. Intellectual Reserve: 2001.

Freud, Sigmund. *Beyond the Pleasure Principle*. Edited by Todd Dufresne and translated by Gregory C. Richter. Broadview, 2011.

General Handbook: Serving in The Church of Jesus Christ of Latter-day Saints. Accessed May 26, 2023. https://www.churchofjesuschrist.org/study/manual/general-handbook.

Gibbon, Edward. *The Decline and Fall of the Roman Empire*. Vol. 1. Alfred A. Knopf, 1994.

Ginzberg, Louis. *The Legends of the Jews*. Vol. 6. The Johns Hopkins University Press, 1998.

Gore, Catherine. *Fascination, and Other Tales*. Vol. 1. Henry Colburn, 1842.

Gottman, John, and Nan Silver. *Why Marriages Succeed or Fail: And How You Can Make Yours Last*. Bloomsbury, 1994.

Hafen, Bruce C. "The Gospel and Romantic Love." BYU Speeches. September 28, 1982. Accessed May 19, 2023. https://speeches.byu.edu/talks/bruce-c-hafen/gospel -romantic-love/.

Herbst Chris M., and John Ichfer. "The Increasing Happiness of US Parents." *Review of Economics of the Household* 14 (2016): 529–51.

Hinckley, Gordon B. "Codes and Covenants." BYU Speeches. October 18, 1994. Accessed April 30, 2023. https:// speeches.byu.edu/talks/gordon-b-hinckley/codes -covenants/.

Holland, Jeffrey R. "Fear Not: Believe Only!" *Liahona*. May 2022.

———. "Of Souls, Symbols, and Sacraments." BYU Speeches. January 12, 1988. Accessed November 30, 2022.

———. "The Other Prodigal." *Ensign*. May 2002.

———. "Personal Purity." *Ensign*. November 1998.

Journal of Discourses. 26 vols. LDS Booksellers Depot, 1854–86.

Kahneman, Daniel, Alan B. Krueger, David A. Schkade, Norbert Schwarz, and Arthur A. Stone. "A Survey Method for Characterizing Daily Life Experience: The Day Reconstruction Method." *Science* 306, no. 5702 (2004): 1776–80.

Kahneman, Daniel. "Objective Happiness." In *Well-Being: The Foundations of Hedonic Psychology*, edited by Daniel Kahneman, Ed Diener, and Norbert Schwarz. Russell Sage Foundation, 1999.

Karris, Robert J. *Eating Your Way Through Luke's Gospel*. Liturgical Press, 2006.

Kierkegaard, Søren. *The Living Thoughts of Kierkegaard*, edited by W. H. Auden. The New York Review of Books, 1999.

Kraus, Nancy, Torbjörn Malmfors, and Paul Slovic. "Intuitive Toxicology: Expert and Lay Judgments of Chemical Risks." In Paul Slovic, *The Perception of Risk*. Routledge, 2000.

"Lesson VI: Ball Room Etiquette." *Usages and Proprieties of Good Society*. In *Young Woman's Journal* 14, no.1 (1903): 46.

Levine, Amy-Jill. *Short Stories by Jesus: The Enigmatic Parables of a Controversial Rabbi*. HarperOne, 2014.

Lewis, C. S. *The Lion, the Witch and the Wardrobe*. Scholastic, 2006.

———. *Mere Christianity*. HarperOne, 2001.

———. *The Screwtape Letters*. HarperCollins, 2001.

Markovits, Daniel. *The Meritocracy Trap: How America's Foundational Myth Feeds Inequality, Dismantles the Middle Class, and Devours the Elite*. Penguin Press, 2019.

Maxwell, Neal A. "'Brim with Joy' (Alma 26:11)." BYU Speeches. January 23, 1996. https://speeches.byu.edu/talks/neal-a-maxwell/brim-joy/.

———. "The Tugs and Pulls of the World." *Ensign*. November 2000.

McKeown, Greg. *Essentialism: The Disciplined Pursuit of Less*. Crown Business, 2014.

Mencken, H. L. *A Mencken Chrestomathy*. Alfred A. Knopf, 1949.

Milton, John. "Paradise Lost." In *Complete Poems and Major Prose*, edited by Merritt Y. Hughes. Hackett Publishing, 2003.

Nelson, Russell M. "Decisions for Eternity." *Ensign*. November 2013.

———. "Let God Prevail." *Ensign*. November 2020.

———. "Overcome the World and Find Rest." *Liahona*. November 2022.

———. "The Sabbath Is a Delight." *Ensign*. May 2015.

Oaks, Dallin H. "Good, Better, Best." *Ensign*. November 2007.

———. "The Great Plan of Happiness." *Ensign*. November 1993.

———. "Revelation." BYU Speeches. September 29, 1981. Accessed October 4, 2022. https://speeches.byu.edu/talks/dallin-h-oaks/revelation/.

———. "Sins and Mistakes." *Liahona* or *Ensign*. October 1996.

Packer, Boyd K. *The Things of the Soul*. Bookcraft, 1996.

Parshall, Ardis E. "Proprieties and Usages of Good Society— Lesson VI. Ball Room Etiquette." March 3, 2010. https://keepapitchinin.org/2010/03/03/proprieties-and-usages-of-good-society-lesson-vi-ball-room-etiquette/.

Pratt, Belinda Marden. *Defence of Polygamy, by a Lady of Utah, in a Letter to Her Sister in New Hampshire.* 1854.

Renlund, Dale G. "A Framework for Personal Revelation." *Liahona.* November 2022.

Rivlin, Lilly. "Lilith." In *Which Lilith? Feminist Writers Re-Create the World's First Woman,* edited by Enid Dame, Lilly Rivlin, and Henny Wenkart. Rowman & Littlefield, 2004.

Robbins, Lynn G. "Until Seventy Times Seven." *Ensign.* May 2018.

Russell, James A. "Introduction: The Return of Pleasure." *Cognition and Emotion* 17, no. 2 (2003): 161–65.

Rytting, Marvin. "Sexual Scripts: Rewriting the Lines." *Exponent II* 9, no. 3 (1983): 16.

Schulz, Kathryn. *Being Wrong: Adventures in the Margin of Error.* HarperCollins, 2010.

Scott, Richard G. "Finding Joy in Life." *Ensign.* May 1996.

Shakespeare, William. *Hamlet.* In *The Complete Works of Shakespeare,* edited by David Bevington. 6th edition. Pearson, 2009.

———. "Sonnet 75." In *The Complete Works of Shakespeare,* edited by David Bevington. 6th edition. Pearson, 2009.

———. *The Taming of the Shrew.* In *The Complete Works of Shakespeare,* edited by David Bevington. 6th edition. Pearson, 2009.

Sill, Sterling W. "Hold Up Your Hands." *Ensign.* May 1973.

Smith, Betty. *A Tree Grows in Brooklyn.* Harper Perennial, 2006.

Smith, Joseph. "Discourse, 30 January 1842." In Wilford Woodruff, *Book of Revelations.* Accessed October 2, 2022. https://www.josephsmithpapers.org/paper-summary/discourse-30-january-1842/2#facts.

———. "Discourse, between circa 26 June and circa 2 July 1839, as Reported by Willard Richards." In Willard Richards, *Journal and Papers.* www.josephsmithpapers.org.

———. *History, 1838–1856, Volume D-1.* Accessed September 20, 2022. https://www.josephsmithpapers.org/.

Uchtdorf, Dieter F. "A Higher Joy." *Liahona.* May 2024.

———. "Your Potential, Your Privilege." *Ensign.* May 2011.

Index

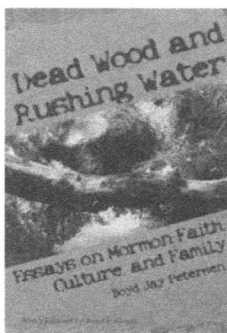

Dead Wood and Rushing Water: Essays on Mormon Faith, Culture, and Family

Boyd Jay Petersen

Paperback, ISBN: 978-1-58958-658-1

For over a decade, Boyd Petersen has been an active voice in Mormon studies and thought. In essays that steer a course between apologetics and criticism, striving for the balance of what Eugene England once called the "radical middle," he explores various aspects of Mormon life and culture—from the Dream Mine near Salem, Utah, to the challenges that Latter-day Saints of the millennial generation face today.

Praise for *Dead Wood and Rushing Water*:

"*Dead Wood and Rushing Water* gives us a reflective, striving, wise soul ruminating on his world. In the tradition of Eugene England, Petersen examines everything in his Mormon life from the gold plates to missions to dream mines to doubt and on to Glenn Beck, Hugh Nibley, and gender. It is a book I had trouble putting down." — Richard L. Bushman, author of *Joseph Smith: Rough Stone Rolling*

"Boyd Petersen is correct when he says that Mormons have a deep hunger for personal stories—at least when they are as thoughtful and well-crafted as the ones he shares in this collection." — Jana Riess, author of *The Twible* and *Flunking Sainthood*

"Boyd Petersen invites us all to ponder anew the verities we hold, sharing in his humility, tentativeness, and cheerful confidence that our paths will converge in the end." — Terryl. L. Givens, author of *People of Paradox: A History of Mormon Culture*

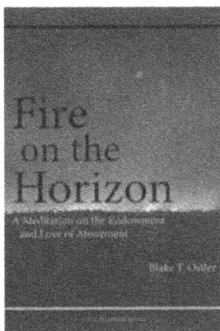

Fire on the Horizon:
A Meditation on the Endowment
and Love of Atonement

Blake T. Ostler

Paperback, ISBN: 978-1-58958-553-9

Blake Ostler, author of the groundbreaking Exploring Mormon Thought series, explores two of the most important and central aspects of Mormon theology and practice: the Atonement and the temple endowment. Utilizing observations from Søren Kierkegaard, Martin Buber, and others, Ostler offers further insights on what it means to become alienated from God and to once again have at-one-ment with Him.

Praise for *Fire on the Horizon*:

"Fire on the Horizon distills decades of reading, argument, and reflection into one potent dose. Urgent, sharp, and intimate, it's Ostler at his best." — Adam S. Miller, author of *Rube Goldberg Machines: Essays in Mormon Theology*

"Blake Ostler has been one of the most stimulating, deep, and original thinkers in the Latter-day Saint community. This book continues and consolidates that status. His work demonstrates that Mormonism can, and indeed does, offer profound nourishment for reflective minds and soul-satisfying insights for thoughtful believers." — Daniel C. Peterson, editor of *Interpreter: A Journal of Mormon Scripture*

Future Mormon:
Essays in Mormon Theology

Adam S. Miller

Paperback, ISBN: 978-1-58958-509-6

From the Introduction:

I have three children, a girl and two boys. Our worlds overlap but, already, these worlds are not the same. Their worlds, the worlds that they will grow to fill, are already taking leave of mine. Their futures are already wedged into our present. This is both heartening and frightening. So much of our world deserves to be left. So much of it deserves to be scrapped and recycled. But, too, this scares me. I worry that a lot of what has mattered most to me in this world—Mormonism in particular—may be largely unintelligible to them in theirs. This problem isn't new, but it is perpetually urgent. Every generation must start again. Every generation must work out their own salvation. Every generation must live its own lives and think its own thoughts and receive its own revelations. And, if Mormonism continues to matter, it will be because they, rather than leaving, were willing to be Mormon all over again. Like our grandparents, like our parents, and like us, they will have to rethink the whole tradition, from top to bottom, right from the beginning, and make it their own in order to embody Christ anew in this passing world. To the degree that we can help, our job is to model that work in love and then offer them the tools, the raw materials, and the room to do it themselves.

These essays are a modest contribution in this vein, a future tense apologetics meant for future Mormons. They model, I hope, a thoughtful and creative engagement with Mormon ideas while sketching, without obligation, possible directions for future thinking.

Whom Say Ye That I Am?
Lessons from
the Jesus of Nazareth

James W. McConkie
and Judith E. McConkie

Paperback, ISBN: 978-1-58958-707-6

"This book is the most important Jesus study to date written by believing Mormons for an LDS audience. It opens the door for Mormons to come to know a Jesus most readers will know little about—the Jesus of history." — David Bokovoy, author of *Authoring the Old Testament: Genesis–Deuteronomy*

"Meticulously documented and researched, the authors have crafted an insightful and enlightening book that allows Jesus to speak by providing both wisdom and council. The McConkies masterfully weave in sources from the Gospels, ancient and modern scholars, along with Christian and non-Christian religious leaders." — *Deseret News*

The story of Jesus is frequently limited to the telling of the babe of Bethlehem who would die on the cross and three days later triumphantly exit his tomb in resurrected glory. Frequently skimmed over or left aside is the story of the Jesus of Nazareth who confronted systemic injustice, angered those in power, risked his life for the oppressed and suffering, and worked to preach and establish the Kingdom of God—all of which would lead to his execution on Calvary.

In this insightful and moving volume, authors James and Judith McConkie turn to the latest scholarship on the historical and cultural background of Jesus to discover lessons on what we can learn from his exemplary life. Whether it be his intimate interactions with the sick, the poor, women, and the outcast, or his public confrontations with oppressive religious, political, and economic institutions, Jesus of Nazareth—the son of a carpenter, Messiah, and Son of God—exemplified the way, the truth, and the life that we must follow to bring about the Kingdom of Heaven.

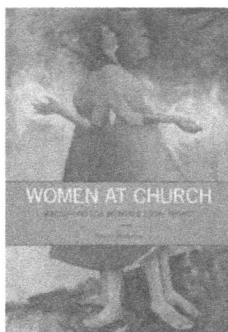

Women at Church:
Magnifying LDS Women's
Local Impact

Neylan McBaine

Paperback, ISBN: 978-1-58958-688-8

Women at Church is a practical and faithful guide to improving the way men and women work together at church. Looking at current administrative and cultural practices, the author explains why some women struggle with the gendered divisions of labor. She then examines ample real-life examples that are currently happening in local settings around the country that expand and reimagine gendered practices. Readers will understand how to evaluate possible pain points in current practices and propose solutions that continue to uphold all mandated church policies. Readers will be equipped with the tools they need to have respectful, empathetic and productive conversations about gendered practices in Church administration and culture.

Praise for *Women at Church*:

"Such a timely, faithful, and practical book! I suggest ordering this book in bulk to give to your bishopric, stake presidency, and all your local leadership to start a conversation on changing Church culture for women by letting our doctrine suggest creative local adaptations—Neylan McBaine shows the way!" — Valerie Hudson Cassler, author of *Women in Eternity, Women of Zion*

"A pivotal work replete with wisdom and insight. Neylan McBaine deftly outlines a workable programme for facilitating movement in the direction of the 'privileges and powers' promised the nascent Female Relief Society of Nauvoo." — Fiona Givens, co-author of *The God Who Weeps: How Mormonism Makes Sense of Life*

"In her timely and brilliant findings, Neylan McBaine issues a gracious invitation to rethink our assumptions about women's public Church service. Well researched, authentic, and respectful of the current Church administrative structure, McBaine shares exciting and practical ideas that address diverse needs and involve all members in the meaningful work of the Church." — Camille Fronk Olson, author of *Women of the Old Testament* and *Women of the New Testament*

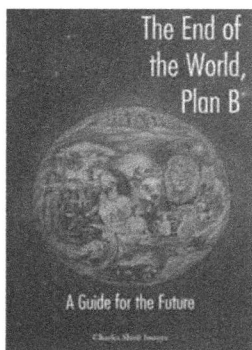

The End of the World, Plan B: A Guide for the Future

Charles Shirō Inouye

Paperback, ISBN: 978-1-58958-755-7

Praise for *End of the World, Plan B*:

"Mormonism needs Inouye's voice. We need, in general, voices that are a bit less Ayn Rand and a bit more Siddhartha Gautama. Inouye reminds us that justice is not enough and that obedience is not the currency of salvation. He urges us to recognize the limits of the law, to see that, severed from a willingness to compassionately suffer with the world's imperfection and evanescence, our righteous hunger for balancing life's books will destroy us all."
— Adam S. Miller, author of *Rube Goldberg Machines: Essays in Mormon Theology* and *Letters to a Young Mormon*

"Drawing on Christian, Buddhist, Daoist, and other modes of thought, Charles Inouye shows how an attitude of hope can arise from a narrative of doom. The End of the World, Plan B is not simply a rethinking of the end of our world, but is a meditation on the possibility of compassionate self-transformation. In a world that looks to the just punishment of the wicked, Inouye shows how sorrow, which comes from the demands of justice, can create peace, forgiveness, and love."
— Michael D.K. Ing, Assistant Professor, Department of Religious Studies, Indiana University

"For years I've hoped to see a book that related Mormonism to the great spiritual traditions beyond Christianity and Judaism. Charles Inouye has done this in one of the best Mormon devotional books I've ever read. His Mormon reading of the fourfold path of the Bodhisattva offers a beautiful eschatology of the end/purpose of the world as the revelation of compassion. I hope the book is read widely."
— James M. McLachlan, co-editor of *Discourses in Mormon Theology: Philosophical and Theological Possibilities*

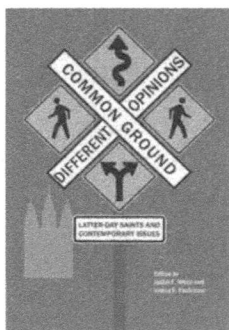

Common Ground—Different Opinions:
Latter-day Saints and Contemporary Issues

Edited by Justin F. White
and James E. Faulconer

Paperback, ISBN: 978-1-58958-573-7

There are many hotly debated issues about which many people disagree, and where common ground is hard to find. From evolution to environmentalism, war and peace to political partisanship, stem cell research to same-sex marriage, how we think about controversial issues affects how we interact as Latter-day Saints.

In this volume various Latter-day Saint authors address these and other issues from differing points of view. Though they differ on these tough questions, they have all found common ground in the gospel of Jesus Christ and the latter-day restoration. Their insights offer diverse points of view while demonstrating we can still love those with whom we disagree.

Praise for *Common Ground—Different Opinions*:

"[This book] provide models of faithful and diverse Latter-day Saints who remain united in the body of Christ. This collection clearly demonstrates that a variety of perspectives on a number of sensitive issues do in fact exist in the Church. . . . [T]he collection is successful in any case where it manages to give readers pause with regard to an issue they've been fond of debating, or convinces them to approach such conversations with greater charity and much more patience. It served as just such a reminder and encouragement to me, and for that reason above all, I recommend this book." — Blair Hodges, Maxwell Institute

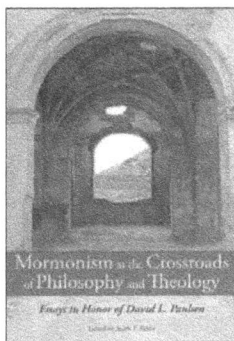

Mormonism at the Crossroads of Philosophy and Theology: Essays in Honor of David L. Paulsen

Edited by Jacob T. Baker

Paperback, ISBN: 978-1-58958-192-0

"There is no better measure of the growing importance of Mormon thought in contemporary religious debate than this volume of essays for David Paulsen. In a large part thanks to him, scholars from all over the map are discussing the questions Mormonism raises about the nature of God and the purpose of life. These essays let us in on a discussion in progress." —RICHARD LYMAN BUSHMAN, author of *Joseph Smith: Rough Stone Rolling*.

"This book makes it clear that there can be no real ecumenism without the riches of the Mormon mind. Professor Paulsen's impact on LDS thought is well known. . . . These original and insightful essays chart a new course for Christian intellectual life." —PETER A. HUFF, and author of *Vatican II* and *The Voice of Vatican II*

"This volume of smart, incisive essays advances the case for taking Mormonism seriously within the philosophy of religion–an accomplishment that all generations of Mormon thinkers should be proud of." —PATRICK Q. MASON, Howard W. Hunter Chair of Mormon Studies, Claremont Graduate University

"These essays accomplish a rare thing—bringing light rather than heat to an on-going conversation. And the array of substantial contributions from outstanding scholars and theologians within and outside Mormonism is itself a fitting tribute to a figure who has been at the forefront of bringing Mormonism into dialogue with larger traditions." —TERRYL L. GIVENS, author of *People of Paradox: A History of Mormon Culture*

"The emergence of a vibrant Mormon scholarship is nowhere more in evidence than in the excellent philosophical contributions of David Paulsen." —RICHARD J. MOUW, President, Fuller Theological Seminary, author of *Talking with Mormons: An Invitation to Evangelicals*

Also available from
GREG KOFFORD BOOKS